HOW TO SAY IT®
for Executives

The Complete Guide to
Communication for Leaders

HOW TO SAY IT®
for Executives

The Complete Guide to Communication for Leaders

Phyllis Mindell

PRENTICE HALL PRESS

THE BERKLEY PUBLISHING GROUP
Published by the Penguin Group
Penguin Group (USA) Inc.
375 Hudson Street, New York, New York 10014, USA
Penguin Group (Canada), 10 Alcorn Avenue, Toronto, Ontario M4V 3B2, Canada
(a division of Pearson Penguin Canada Inc.)
Penguin Books Ltd., 80 Strand, London WC2R 0RL, England
Penguin Group Ireland, 25 St. Stephen's Green, Dublin 2, Ireland (a division of Penguin Books Ltd.)
Penguin Group (Australia), 250 Camberwell Road, Camberwell, Victoria 3124, Australia
(a division of Pearson Australia Group Pty. Ltd.)
Penguin Books India Pvt. Ltd., 11 Community Centre, Panchsheel Park, New Delhi—110 017, India
Penguin Group (NZ), Cnr. Airborne and Rosedale Roads, Albany, Auckland 1310, New Zealand
(a division of Pearson New Zealand Ltd.)
Penguin Books (South Africa) (Pty.) Ltd., 24 Sturdee Avenue, Rosebank, Johannesburg 2196,
South Africa

Penguin Books Ltd., Registered Offices: 80 Strand, London WC2R 0RL, England

This book is an original publication of The Berkley Publishing Group.

Copyright © 2005 by Phyllis Mindell
Cover design by Jill Boltin
Text design by Tiffany Estreicher
Cover art by Felix Sockwell

PRINTING HISTORY
Prentice Hall Press paperback edition: January 2005

Library of Congress Cataloging-in-Publication Data

Mindell, Phyllis.
How to say it for executives : the complete guide to communicating for leaders / by Phyllis Mindell.
p. cm.
Includes bibliographical references.
ISBN 0-7352-0388-1
1. Business communication. 2. Executives. I. Title.

HF5718.M549 2005
658.4'5—dc22   2004053539

PRINTED IN THE UNITED STATES OF AMERICA

10 9 8 7 6 5 4 3

To Samuel Ephraim Borosh Mindell

What distinguishes leaders . . . is that they find a voice that allows them to articulate the common dream.

—WARREN BENNIS

CONTENTS

Acknowledgments   xi

Preface   xiii

Introduction   xv

1. Seminal Ideas   1

2. Leading Your Self   12

3. Reading Like a Leader   18

4. Listening Like a Leader   31

5. Leading Without Words: Presence, Charisma, and
   Nonverbal Communications   46

6. Talking Like a Leader   58

7. Building Sturdy Structures   85

8. Organizing Spoken and Written Communications   101

9. Addressing Your Public   106

10. Delivering Speeches that Lead   116

11. Communicating with Small Groups and Individuals   125

12. Writing Like a Leader   142

13. Bridging Cultures—Toward a Language of
    Community in a Diverse Workplace   156

Conclusion   169

Appendix   171

Index   181

About the Author   189

ACKNOWLEDGMENTS

Thanks and acknowledgment go to the thousands of executives and professionals who generously shared their stories and experiences. If this book makes sense it's because of their integrity and honesty. Invaluable counsel has also come from Roberta Schwartz, Kathleen Barry Albertini, Ron Mix, Marlene Maggio, Vicki Casarett, Stacey Freed, and Jennifer Hutchins. The love and support of family and friends inspire all my creative work. Thanks to all of you. And the joy of watching language unfold in my beloved grandchildren, Arye and Sam, has deepened my respect for the great miracles of growth and learning.

PREFACE

For a quarter century, I've worked with people on the way to or in executive suites and other leadership positions, coming from or working in nearly every country and from every social and educational background. My students range from the CEO of an international manufacturing firm to the dean of a medical school to the undergraduate who leads the Muslim Association at a university. They share two traits: all seek excellence in their fields and all seek to lead wisely, humanely, and ethically. And despite varied styles, strategies, and situations, all accepted the centrality of language in their quests.

This book offers leaders and future leaders all the information and skill required to communicate whatever messages they create to any audiences they address. It does not seek to impose a common mold, philosophy, style, or strategy—other writers cited here have done so ably and everyone should read their works. My goal is to endow you with what you need to communicate in every leadership situation, from listening effectively to persuading the hostile to transforming the naysayer to gleaning information to giving light in times of crisis. *How to Say It for Executives* grew from the insights of executives, managers, doctors, lawyers, teachers, scientists, politicians, and others. I read great thinkers and sought to absorb and synthesize their ideas. I analyzed thousands of speeches, letters, and e-mails. I scoured research for relevant studies.

But mostly I tapped my own experience and those of thousands of adults who have studied with me over the years. Every story in this book is true—every word was said, every speech was written, although details or circumstances were sometimes altered to protect my sources. The only people named are well-known historical, business, and political figures and experts who so graciously aided my writing. When I speak about political language and its successes or failings, my purpose is not to comment on politics, only on language.

And language matters. This book went to press during a presidential campaign, the outcome of which was influenced by the candidates' words. As Professor Stanley Fish noted in the *New York Times*, "Words are not just the cosmetic clothing of some underlying integrity; they are the operational vehicles of that integrity, the visible manifestation of the character to which others respond. And if the words you use fall apart, ring hollow, trail off . . . , the suspicion will grow that what they lack is what you lack, and no one will follow." Enjoy your leadership quest, laugh at your missteps, encourage laughter in others, and keep your eye on the goal. I wish you every success and many good words.

—Phyllis Mindell, Ed.D.

INTRODUCTION

Congratulations! You've made it into the executive suite, the boardroom, the professional office, the political role, the leadership job, or the consultant's seat. That's the good news—the bad news is that you must lead. You must give speeches. You must establish authority. You must persuade. You must negotiate. You must inspire, motivate, foster growth in others. You must participate on teams. You must deal with obnoxious people. You must comfort in hard times. In short, you must gain followers. Yet if you're like most of my students, your education, experience, and training have ill prepared you to go beyond your professional domain. *How to Say It for Executives* is here to rescue you. It's the complete guide to every aspect of leadership communication: a trove of ideas, specifics, step-by-step instructions, models, checklists, even How to Say It sections of exact words to say in challenging situations. And it's organized to meet the needs of the busy leader; after you've read the first chapters, you can proceed straight to the section that addresses your immediate concerns.

An Overview of *How to Say It for Executives*

After the Introduction in which you consider the language skills you use every day at work, you'll meet ideas that gird the practical applications. Among them: leadership is not a static phenomenon but rather a fluid series of challenges; leadership emerges in a more or less predictable developmental pattern; the four levels of *novice, apprentice, master,* and *mentor* offer a convenient way to map your growth; embracing paradox helps avoid oversimplification regarding the skills in this book; no one leadership "style" works in every situation; three fundamental questions help you craft successful communications; models and specific words guide you till you've mastered the approaches learned here; actual, fictional, and historical leaders offer models to follow as you craft a personal leadership presence.

The next chapter, "Leading Your Self," discusses the essential self-understanding and self-regulation that enable you to control your behavior. "Reading Like a Leader" and "Listening Like a Leader" provide the critical receptive language skills that empower you to learn quickly and efficiently, whether from printed sources or by word of mouth. "Leading Without Words" covers nonverbal language in detail, from the top of your head to the soles of your feet. After that, "Talking Like a Leader" introduces what you must know about sentences that fail or work, rhetorical tools, persuasion, critique, and word choices. "Building Sturdy Structures" that likens the construction of spoken and written communications to the construction of buildings and shows structures that speed the planning process. "Organizing Spoken and Written Communications" walks through a quick, effective way to design messages of all kinds.

Everyone who leads must stand before audiences; "Addressing Your Public" and "Delivering Speeches That Lead" give vital information that aids success, whether you speak to audiences of ten or ten thousand. But the executive suite also requires informal conversations at meetings, with difficult people, for individuals, during critiques, and as a mentor. "Communicating With Small Groups and Individuals" covers these challenging encounters. The executive suite also demands careful, precise, even inspiring written pieces. After telling sad stories of written communications that wreaked havoc, "Writing Like a Leader" takes you on a journey to the Seven Cs of Executive Writing.

Finally, *How to Say It for Executives*'s model of language offers a way to bridge cultures within a company and across the world. "Bridging Cultures— Toward a Language of Community in a Diverse Workplace" takes you on the first steps toward the "creation of the beloved community." Finally, the Guideposts in the Appendix detail all the skills in *How to Say It for Executives*. Familiarize yourself with the guideposts now; they map your growth, remind you of communication essentials, and help you assess your emerging mastery.

Before You Begin

According to several Harvard case studies that track the workdays of CEOs, the schedule for a typical leader apportions the day as follows: 20 percent reading, 20 percent writing (dictating and word processing), 40 percent formal presentations (includes listening and speaking informally), and 30 percent informal meetings (involving speaking and listening). These figures add up to more than 100 percent because the communications overlap. CEOs (and you probably) also spend travel time communicating—speaking on the phone; reading books, proposals, and periodicals; and dictating or writing on a laptop.

Now think about how you spend *your* workdays. Record all your activity in a typical business day (if you have enough help, have an aide track you). Keep a bullet list, and start each item with a verb. For example, your list might look like this:

- Read e-mail.

- Check headlines on Web.

- Open snail mail.

- Read three articles.

- Meet with aides.

- Attend board meeting.

- Present quarterly plan.

- Lunch with largest customer.

- Rehearse speech for international conference.

- Commend high performers for quarter.

- Dictate letter to government agency.

- Take limo to airport while using cell phone to call problem suppliers.

- Catch 5 p.m. flight to conference.

- Write and read e-mail on airplane.

Now check each item that requires one or more language skill—all? Ninety percent? The higher you rise, the larger the percent of your time you will spend communicating. Yet you studied to be an engineer or a doctor or an accountant or a marketer, not to be a communicator. That's why you're reading this book.

1

SEMINAL IDEAS

Ideas are a dime a dozen. People who implement them are price-
less.
                                                    —MARY KAY ASH

Ideas do not spring from writers' brains—they grow from exposure to the ideas of others: emerging from experience, they transform to meet new requirements. By the time the ideas venture into the world, they may lose their origins in the thoughts of others. The ideas in this book present my blend of other thinkers' work with my own experience; if you find these thoughts about language interesting, you may want to revisit the thinkers who inspired them.

Much of this chapter links to the work of Howard Gardner, whose book *Leading Minds*[1] recognizes that leadership is not static but a fluid, emerging series of challenges and issues that follow a predictable developmental pattern. In his study, Gardner traced common elements in the lives of men and women who led in varied fields and countries. The element that emerged most strongly was communications ability: every leader in every sphere from every part of the world possessed powerful language abilities. These abilities surfaced early and flourished as the leader matured. Gardner encourages us to think of the leader as "a storyteller." He notes that leaders must "know their stories, to get them straight, to communicate them effectively . . . and, above all, to embody in their lives the stories that they tell." This book offers the abilities to think through your story, tell it wisely, and craft new stories as your leadership skills grow.

---

[1]Gardner, Howard, *Leading Minds: An Anatomy of Leadership*. New York: Basic Books, 1995.

Stages of Leadership Development

Consider that leadership emerges in a more or less predictable developmental pattern, that you can evaluate your level of ability in various aspects, and that you can choose to advance skills that you and your audiences value. Each level brings new challenges. These challenges and levels are independent of your domain expertise: you can be a superb engineer yet find yourself totally unprepared to address the International Engineering Association meeting in Lisbon. For convenience, let's consider four levels and link them to their language manifestations, and then use these levels to assess the various skills. This section pursues ideas that appeared for the first time in *How to Say It for Women*[2] and in speeches to various audiences since then.

NOVICE PERSPECTIVES

Start with the novice. The beginning leader shows promise but has not yet found a voice. This stage may or may not link to age. Novice leaders enrich every group in which they participate, whether the typing pool or the voluntary society. One novice leader, a successful scientist, was made dean of a medical school. At fifty, she was a novice at leadership and had to learn a whole new set of communication skills. Another, an undergraduate, heads the Muslim student group at a university. He struggles to make his ideas heard. Surveys of my clients show this sense of inexperience at every level. One person wrote that, "I was used to battling to get resources for my own work; now suddenly I must support everyone else's work as well." If the fledgling leader is young, the language shows promising early traits (as noted by Gardner): "speaks skillfully, shows keen interest in other people, [has] general energy and resourcefulness, [is] willing to confront authority, takes risks, shows concern with moral issues, is competitive, enjoys achieving a position of control."

The novice leader asks: "How shall I craft my persona?" "How shall I nurture my natural skills?" "How can I draw attention to my promise?" "Whom

---

[2]Mindell, Phyllis, *How to Say It for Women*. New York: Prentice Hall, 2001.

shall I seek to mentor me?" "What role models illuminate the path before me?" This promising leader seeks to learn and refine communication skills such as:

- Building an excellent reference library

- Reading widely and beyond own field

- Gaining experience in speaking in small and informal settings

- Listening intently

- Perfecting fundamentals of grammar and style

- Seeking appropriate external support, mentoring, and education

- Offering to organize and lead small groups and meetings

- Informing critical decision-makers that you seek leadership opportunities

When you assess your skills by using the Guideposts in the back of this book, consider yourself a novice if the skill is new to you.

APPRENTICE

The American Heritage Dictionary defines *apprentice* as "one who is learning a trade or occupation." We acknowledge that the apprentice is learning to lead others rather than simply showing promise. He or she might lead a small group, start a neighborhood association, or have moved into a middle management job. The young tenured professor, the engineering team leader, the assistant vice president, the new department chair may all be apprentice leaders.

The apprentice must stand prepared for the cycle of success, failure, and renewal that is the lot of all leaders. If the apprentice chooses to learn how to lead, she or he must broaden the sphere and communicate with larger groups. As you advance through the apprentice stage, continue to enhance the skills you started as a novice, and add advanced language and leadership skills such as:

- Increasing efficiency in using the Web to gather advanced information

- Writing clearly not only for professionals but for a widening audience

- Volunteering for challenging presentation opportunities

- Acquiring the principles of rhetoric and persuasion

- Cultivating rhetorical skills

- Addressing larger audiences

- Being yourself in a way that earns respect

- Continuing to seek and work with mentors

- Continuing the lifelong habit of risk-taking

- Modeling ideas through behavior

- Following Ralph Waldo Emerson's dictate, "Always do what you are afraid to do."

Concerning the guideposts in this book, you're an apprentice if you have the rudiments of the behavior and aim for mastery.

MASTER

The master is a seasoned leader. The master has known real success: peers and followers accept you as a leader. The job title may be president, director, vice president. As a master you have a well-defined sense of yourself, both strengths and weaknesses. Leadership poses large issues for masters; they must make the opportunity for reflection, see the big picture. The seasoned leader moves onto ever larger stages. Talks no longer address small or affinity groups but large, perhaps international, audiences. Meetings no longer comprise peers alone but professionals from other disciplines and the public. Persuasion no longer operates in the area of expertise alone but reaches out beyond. Language must include sharing a vision, encouraging others, rewarding success, nurturing young leaders. Reading no longer seeks just the professional journal in your own field but books and articles about the wider world and about leadership itself. Writing goes beyond data and proposals to plain-language descriptions that reach out to varied audiences. Television appearances may be required, as well as press interviews. You now give voice to the "stories" and aspirations of the group. As a master, you know how to apply your communication skills to run successful meetings, manage others, work with customers, lead growing organizations, and balance the everyday paradoxes of life. Warren Bennis notes, "What distinguishes leaders . . . is that they find a voice that allows them to articulate the common dream." Gardner talks of the seasoned leader's "charisma, flexibility, capacity to adjust stories to changing circumstances while remaining an individual of conviction." And, always, the master grapples with the risk of failure. You have grown tough, robust, energized by setbacks, and you return to the fray with a new vigor, construing every defeat as an opportunity.

In short, the master manages language and communication to advance the leadership agenda.

MENTOR

But a higher level of leadership beckons, not for everyone but for a select few who continue to stretch and grow, beyond the career, beyond the domain, beyond the personal. Let's call this level the *mentor*. Do you know the origin of the word? It comes from the *Odyssey,* in which a wise old man named Mentor counsels Odysseus's son while his father is at sea. Of course, Mentor was actually the goddess Athena come to earth in the guise of an old man, so mentor carries both masculine and feminine identity.

As I see them, mentors no longer concern themselves with career, earnings, and gaining followers; they have moved beyond daily local issues to play their roles on a larger stage. They may earn national leadership, often beyond their original expertise. I added mentor to the guidepost levels to acknowledge a group of leaders with whom I have had the privilege of working: the dean of a medical school who now travels the world persuading countries to adopt policies that reduce AIDS, the ninety-five-year-old psychotherapist who still mentors me, the successful attorney who has started free legal clinics.

And even the mentor deals with recurring communication issues: how to inspire a shared vision, how to get people to rise above their narrow interests, how to refine the already strong voice, how to craft a "story" that conveys the message even farther from the intimate circle. Even if you have attained this highest level, you seek to grow your skills.

Janus Paradoxes

Face it: we bring a tangled web of emotions, intellect, and skills to a tangled world of people and places. It would be a blessing if this book could lay out seven or ten or even one hundred principles or rules or styles that would make everyone communicate and lead successfully. But that's not the way it works. For every practice in this book that has worked successfully for thousands of people, we can think of situations in which it would utterly fail. That's why psychologists say psychology holds no truths. This book also holds no absolute truths: take it all with a grain of salt and a large dose of common sense and ask yourself if each idea will work with your personality, your style, your situation, and your audience.

To avoid oversimplification, consider the Roman god Janus, who is always presented with two heads or two faces, each representing the opposite of the other. For example, Janus is the god of peace and of war, the god of entrances and exits, of endings and beginnings, of past and future. So Janus offers us a fine symbol of the paradoxes in language: in any one situation my solution may work best, or its opposite may work best. Each of us has within us a powerful leader and a terrified follower. Any circumstance might demand a democratic leader or an autocratic leader. Some problems can best be solved by a team while others require one decision maker.

The physicist Niels Bohr noted, "The opposite of a correct statement is a false statement. The opposite of a profound yes may well be another profound truth." That's why those personality surveys lead to such paradoxical results: no one is a pure leader or a pure follower; each of us can sometimes lead and sometimes follow. Indeed, in *Team Talk*[3], Ann Donnellon actually uses the term *paradox* to describe the inherent dualities of teamwork. She speaks of four "common paradoxes of group life: the paradox of individual-

---

[3]Donnellon, Ann, *Team Talk: The Power of Language in Team Dynamics*. Boston: Harvard Business School Press, 1996.

ity, the paradox of identity, the paradox of interdependence, and the paradox of trust."

Paul Schulman, Kathryn Hannon Professor of Government at Mills College, has studied the problems of what he calls the "trade-off between ambiguity and specificity in the world of organization."[4] He notes, "More and more of the work of organizations is being conducted under formalized models, regulations, procedures, and standards . . . expressed in the seeming precision of artificial language . . . in contrast to natural language, with its evolved usage and inevitable ambiguities . . . The spread of formality represents the ascendancy of the values of specificity, precision, and completeness over those of flexibility, discretion, and trust. . . . We so often stress the value of clarity in communication, but what about the reciprocal skill of keeping certain things deliberately imprecise and ambiguous?" Control this Janus paradox through perfection of your "natural language."

Do It Now!

The executive suite brings a plethora of Janus paradoxes. On the list below, check those you face at work and add others.

- ❑ **Empowerment versus control**

- ❑ **Speak for oneself versus speak for one's company**

- ❑ **Coach versus play on team**

- ❑ **Make snap decisions versus carefully reasoned decisions**

- ❑ **Look to the past versus the future**

- ❑ **Seek short-term versus long-term goals**

- ❑ **Employee benefits versus profits**

- ❑ **Domain versus leadership skill**

---

[4]Unpublished letter, July 16, 1997.

❑ Autonomy versus collaboration

❑ Individuality versus "groupthink"

❑ Unity versus diversity

❑ Democracy versus autocracy

❑ Shared versus individual decision-making

In sum, beware that your search for simplicity doesn't lead to simplemindedness. Don't just accept but welcome complexity when you lead.

The Question of Leadership Style

"Style" has grown stylish: articles, books, and assessments seek to evaluate leadership style, discuss it, alter it. Yet any review of history reveals that successful leaders take on various styles: both Attila the Hun and Mother Teresa can succeed. Still, whichever style works for you, you must control its expression in language and be sure it brings success. My files are full of stories of leaders who fell because employees or clients or the public resented their style. If you have a notoriously abrasive style, soften its language expression; if you have a laid-back style, learn to express it more powerfully.

Adjust the style to changing circumstances. One of my clients, a truck driver who eventually owned a large fleet, was invited to address his national trade association. As he worked on his talk, he resisted the notion that it was not appropriate to discuss how he "kicked ass" to get where he was or how he once found himself "ass deep" in snow. Adhere to the highest levels of civility (remember: you're the model). But, beyond that, remain true to yourself and your ethical principles.

Three Questions

Even in the face of the Janus paradoxes, this book offers general principles in the form of questions that guide you through your verbal language choices.

The first question asks, "What is it *not* about?" That's a strange language principle. Why must you ascertain what you're *not* talking about? The reason: English speakers expect to hear the subject of a sentence at or near its beginning. Yet the thousands of sentences and transcripts in my file reveal that most people begin most sentences with the word "I," both in writing and in speaking. These "I" statements suggest that you're talking about yourself all the time, which you did not intend to do.

As we discuss various language challenges, *you'll see the problems of leaders who haven't figured out that leadership is not about the leader—it's about the problem, the ideas, the principles, the strategies, and the audience.*

Now you have every right to shout, "This is ridiculous! Of course it's about me! I'm the boss!" Or you may have been told that you should take ownership of your words. Yes, do take ownership, but not by using the weak "I" statement. Or you could object, "But I'm the most interesting thing in my life." Yes, we're each the most interesting thing in our own lives—we think about ourselves all the time. The problem comes when we decide we're the most interesting thing in everyone else's lives, as in the old joke, "We've talked about me enough; let's talk about you. Tell me, what do you think of me?" People who talk about themselves all the time bore everyone; that's not the way to engage followers. Sometimes they talk about themselves as a way of dominating others (we'll talk about that later) but most of us aren't that savvy—we simply like to talk about ourselves.

If they're ever to speak again, leaders must next ask the second question, "What *am* I talking about?" Or, "What is the subject of this sentence?" Then they open the sentence with its subject. We'll elaborate on this fundamental principle as we get to the applications and models.

The third question asks, "What does it do?" Now that the sentence has a subject, it needs a verb. We'll detail the key role of the verb and give you lots of practice and examples later. For now, choose action (go, help, speak, consider, agree) rather than "to be" verbs (is, am, are).

You now have a sentence that doesn't talk about you, talks about something that matters, and contains an all-important action verb. Just finish the statement.

The fourth question asks, "How does it link?" Will this sentence just hang or will it have a logical link to what preceded and what follows? Leaders who wish to persuade must show the relationships among ideas and facts. We'll detail many ways to link ideas in the following chapters of this book.

HOW TO SAY IT

Even if you fully understand the principles and the questions, it won't be easy to apply them on the spot. The notion of the *How to Say It* crib sheets emerged the day a friend called to say that she dreaded a difficult meeting scheduled for the next day. She predicted the awful things people would say and asked me to help her figure out how to respond so she could arrive prepared. Thousands of my students and readers have benefitted from the *How to Say It* crib sheets in earlier books—not forever but until they felt comfortable constructing their own sentences, speeches, and replies. They should serve you as well.

MODELS

Amateur writers imitate. Professionals steal. It's not enough to understand the language principles; you want models that show step-by-step how to construct speeches, memos, letters, and visuals. You'll find them throughout this book. Copy what's useful to you, changing only the content words.

FOLLOW THE LEADERS

Finally, no one works in a vacuum. Just as artists imitate other artists as they seek their own styles, so leaders imitate those they admire as they craft their leadership styles. You'll find great and famous people cited in this book, but don't neglect the role models found in fiction, film, at home, even in the next cubicle. Successful leaders I've interviewed tell of lessons they learned from parents, relatives, friends, teachers, and coworkers. So find leaders you admire and look to them for lessons, not just general but specific lessons. Watch an admired person at a meeting and note words, voice, body language, and eye contact. Borrow tapes of great speeches from the library and determine what you can emulate. Read excellent reports and copy sentences.

Do It Now!

Estimate your level on each of the skills in the guideposts. Ask staff and superiors to do so for you as well. Compare the scores. If your self-assessments match those of the others, you show strong self-awareness. Decide which skills you wish to develop now and which to develop later.

2

LEADING YOUR SELF

To thine own self be true, And it must follow as the night the day, thou canst not then be false to any man. . . .

—William Shakespeare

Before deciding how to lead others, decide how to lead your self. The recommendations in this book require that you control every aspect of your language. Whether it's the decision on how to hold your head and body or the decision on how to handle a difficult audience, success depends on managing what to say and how to say it. So before tackling the individual skills, look into your self—the self that shapes your language.

WELCOME RISK

To paraphrase Harry Truman's famous words, the buck really does stop here. In entering the executive suite, you've taken on a risky job, one undoubtedly far more risky than the one you left. If you fear risk, if the possibility of failure paralyzes you, change jobs. Gardner's and Bennis's[5] studies of leaders show that they all fail at critical points in their development. Indeed, Gardner speaks of the "recurrent cycle of failure and renewal."

If, however, you stand ready to grapple with fear of failure, indeed of failure itself, then you're well prepared to lead. In Eleanor Roosevelt's words,

---

[5]Op. cit.

"You gain strength, courage, and confidence by every experience in which you really stop to look fear in the face. . . . You must do the thing you cannot do."

SEEK CRITIQUE FROM A VARIETY OF PERSPECTIVES

If you've decided that you're a wonderful leader, that's great. But check to see if those with whom you work think so too. To ensure that managers get criticism from various perspectives, companies ask customers, staff, and peers to evaluate them. The results can prove an unpleasant awakening if other people's perspectives fail to match yours. Use commercially available 360 Assessments or the Guideposts at the back of this book to check the match. *How to Say It for Executives* Guideposts offer the opportunity to let leaders know in an unthreatening way how they're perceived. For example, one French executive asked her staff to evaluate her on the Guideposts and found out that her staff considered her a master at numerous skills but a novice at delegating. After seeing the assessments, she could rethink her delegating approach without feeling beleaguered.

Solicit Information and Views of Others

Upon the death of President Ronald Reagan, Mikhail Gorbachev wrote of him, "While adhering to his convictions, with which one could agree or disagree, he was not dogmatic; he was looking for negotiation and cooperation." If the leader of the free world could solicit the views of others, you can too.

"Thinks he knows everything" never appears in lists of leadership attributes. Your job requires assimilation and synthesis of the group's collective knowledge and wisdom. It will come to you only if you seek it. This book shows how to solicit the views of others without demeaning them or yourself.

LEARN FROM MISTAKES, GAIN SELF-CONFIDENCE
THROUGH EXPERIENCE

These two march hand in hand. Mistake-free means learning-free and growth-free. Of course you and your staff will err. Learn from those errors. And don't even try to teach self-confidence, it comes from learning new skills, experiencing both success and failure. A famous, and very public, failure happened to William Jefferson Clinton while he was governor of Arkansas. As a featured speaker at the Democratic convention, he rambled in a too long and too dull speech whose only applause line was "In conclusion. . . ." After this public failure, he learned excellent public speaking skills and won the presidency. President Bush also tasted public failures when, after the terrorist attacks of 2001, he referred to the murderers as "folks." He too learned.

EXERCISE SELF-AWARENESS AND SELF-REGULATION

Daniel Goleman, who coined the term *emotional intelligence*, cites attributes that differentiate successful leaders from others of equal intelligence and skill.[6] The first two attributes of emotional intelligence include *self-awareness* and *self-regulation*. Goleman says that "people with strong self-awareness are neither overly critical nor unrealistically hopeful. Rather, they are honest—with themselves and with others. People who have a high degree of self-awareness recognize how their feelings affect them, other people, and their job performance."

In Well-Read's leadership seminars, we ask participants to evaluate their own and others' performances and to subject themselves to outside evaluations. It's not uncommon to get reactions like, "Oh god, it's horrible," "I'll never get up to speak again," or "I'm a terrible speaker [or writer or leader]." Such self-evaluations hinder growth and development; they reveal a *lack* of self-awareness. In contrast, if you look at your own performance, judge strengths and weaknesses accurately, and understand and prepare for your own "hot button" issues, you're well on the way to self-awareness.

The principle "It's not about you" encourages you to avoid constantly talking about yourself. But understanding that it's not about you doesn't mean you avoid self-understanding or even that you never talk about your own feelings and attitudes; indeed, I urge you to choose language forms that give voice to your passions and ideas, but to do so in a powerful and mature way.

How can you attain self-awareness? Many tools and many routes to self-awareness can help: yoga, meditation, psychological evaluation and counsel-

---

[6] Goleman, Daniel, "What Makes a Leader?" *Harvard Business Review* (November–December 1998) pp. 93–102.

ing, books, support groups, and coaching. If you can't afford or don't want professional help, take time to view yourself as if you were an outsider (Asking outsiders also works). And take time to explore the many avenues of self-awareness.

Clinical psychologists interviewed for this book find that people who seem out of touch with their own feelings and abilities often suffer from a sense of inadequacy or an inappropriate drive to control others. They also misread situations, act precipitously when faced with challenges, and find it hard to judge people. For example, Dr. Evelyn Abrams, a psychotherapist, described a patient who rose high in his company but was judged a poor leader and found little satisfaction in his work or life. With the guidance of his therapist, he saw that lack of a college degree made him feel ashamed; he tried to make up for it by blustering and acting superior. As he came to terms with his abilities as well as his weaknesses, he accepted himself and learned to accept the strengths and weaknesses of those who reported to him. When his fears no longer haunted his every act, he gained not only self-confidence but the confidence of others.

Another psychotherapist discusses ways in which unresolved events from long ago can "sneak up from behind your head," "speak through you," and get you to behave like an automaton. How do you know if this happens to you? If you react inappropriately to situations, if you blow up in fury at a slight offense, if you can't control your temper, if you rule through fear and intimidation, if your anxiety mismatches the situation, if you're afraid to speak in public, if you can't handle disagreement, if you fail to show compassion, you may mindlessly repeat behaviors that come from childhood and don't work for an adult who leads. Evaluate your performance and observe how others respond to you.

Self-regulation, of course, relies on self-understanding. You can't make fear or hostile feelings go away but you can and must regulate and control their expression. The boss who explodes in rage may win fear but won't win followers. Self-regulation is evident in armed-forces news conferences: soft-spoken generals and admirals win our respect and willingness to listen even when they talk about ugly and brutal situations.

A few years ago, a call came in from a senior executive describing her clinical depression. Her brilliance at work allowed her to succeed despite long years of depression and several suicide attempts. But the dark personality interfered with her ability to persuade clients. I explained that I'm not a psychiatrist or a clinical psychologist and could not treat the depression but that I could help with the regulation of her behavior. We agreed to try a consultation. She slouched into my office wearing her usual dark, sternly tailored suit and severe haircut. Her nonverbal and verbal demeanor suggested nothing but sadness. After learning to watch herself critically on videotape, she determined to alter her body language, speak more positively to and about her clients, and choose bright, cheerful clothes on her darkest days. Two weeks later, she called to tell about a routine meeting she'd run, after which people asked if she'd had therapy. Self-regulation hadn't cured the depression but had enabled her to manage it successfully.

Self-regulation also involves telling the truth about yourself when appropriate and necessary. That doesn't mean saying, "I feel good about . . ." or "I feel bad about . . ." or talking about yourself all the time. It *does* mean openness about your concerns and expression of your passions.

Mindful learning, another aspect of self-regulation, is detailed in the work of psychologist Ellen Langer.[7] Langer describes a mindful approach to any activity as having three characteristics: "the continuous creation of new categories, openness to new information, and an implicit awareness of more than one perspective." In contrast, mindlessness "is characterized by an entrapment in old categories, by automatic behavior that precludes attending to new signals, and by action that operates from a single perspective." By now you no longer operate from a single perspective and may have begun to free yourself of old categories about leadership. Langer describes research showing that slight changes in instructions, from absolute to conditional, alter the way people learn and understand. For example, in one study students were "introduced to a set of objects either conditionally ("This could be a . . .") or in absolute form ("This is a . . ."). Those who heard the conditional introduction learned the basic skill equally well but went on to shape creative uses of the objects while the others did not. In sum, mindful learning and speaking promise to add nuance to your leadership communications.

---

[7]Langer, Ellen, *The Power of Mindful Learning.* Reading, MA: Perseus, 1997.

Do It Now!

Start a diary of language encounters that work or fail, to help you determine whether old experiences are sneaking up and speaking through you. Videotape a meeting you run and view tape of yourself and meeting participants. Evaluate your self-regulation and mindfulness.

As you progress toward mastery in leading yourself, you'll grow in ability to lead others. Intrinsic to that growth is the ability to learn efficiently and apply those learnings to the work of leadership. The most efficient way to learn is, of course, reading.

3

READING LIKE A LEADER

But if men are human because they can talk, they are civilized because they can read.

—DAN LACY

Garbage in, garbage out. It's not just true for research data; it's true for leaders as well. Strategies count, tactics count, and human relations count. But in the end, the quality of your leadership relies on reading. This was true in the middle ages when few books were available; it was true in the twentieth century when millions of books were available; and it's true today when books, articles, letters, newspapers, magazines, journals, and Web pages overwhelm us. Your success as a leader mirrors the quality of your language; the quality of your language mirrors the quality and quantity of your reading. This chapter explores the essential role of reading in leadership, lays out the principles and techniques of Speed, Power, and E-reading, and offers dozens of suggestions to help you manage the reading load as you seek to lead wisely and effectively.

Why reading? Read any biography of a leader; almost invariably it speaks of an early and sustained interest in reading. In his autobiography, Jean-Paul Sartre describes his yearning to read, which arose from the constant repetition of his favorite stories. He wrote, "I witnessed the . . . eternal recurrence of names and events." Alberto Manguel opens his history of reading[8] with the history of his own reading. A colleague and I polled Nobel laureate scientists to ask about what influenced their choice of career. Every one of them de-

---

[8]Manguel, Albert, *A History of Reading*. New York: Viking, 1996.

scribed *Microbe Hunters* as the inspiration. When scientist Rosalind Yalow won the Nobel prize, she said that it was Marie Curie's biography that inspired her career choice. Lincoln famously read the Bible and used it to inspire his language, as did Martin Luther King, Jr.

Slave owners and tyrants have always known that reading offers a path to power; that's why it was a crime to teach slaves to read in the South before the Civil War. When Malcolm X arrived in jail, he was illiterate. He learned to read there and wrote in his autobiography, "as my word-base broadened, I could for the first time pick up a book and read and now begin to understand what the book was saying. Anyone who has read a great deal can imagine the new world that opened. I never had been so truly free in my life." In prison he came to see illiteracy as a second, inner jail that could confine him forever. Reading freed him to take on his leadership role. If you can read but don't, you join the millions of *aliterates* who lock themselves in that same inner jail, and constrain your leadership potential. But reading doesn't just yield ideas and powerful language—it enables you to learn quickly. Except for a few disciplines that are acquired best by watching a master or a videotape, reading is the fastest, cheapest, most efficient way to learn—and you must learn a lot to ace the executive suite.

Through history, books were rare and unavailable to most people. That shortage enabled those who read to form a natural community—a few people read the same few books and shared a common experience. Now the ready availability of books, combined with the miracle of the World Wide Web, brings the world's wisdom into our offices. Yet we drift, lost in cyberspace. Like the parched one who reaches the oasis only to drown in its watery abundance, we drown in the surfeit of information on paper and on the Web. We, who thought we knew how to read and have mastered the texts of our own disciplines, suddenly find ourselves with more to read, less time to read it, and greater demands on our ability to understand and apply new information to our leadership work.

A survey of graduate students at MIT, future leaders in their fields, revealed that most complained of advanced problems such as reading too slowly or too fast, losing attention, and failing to retain. They aimed to synthesize, read critically, retain more, gain efficiency, and work more effectively in cyberspace. And I do not meet an executive or professional who doesn't complain of an inability to keep up with necessary reading, let alone reading that helps to lead. Yet you are what you read.

The Speed and Power Reading System

The Speed and Power Reading System[9] meets the needs of executives and professionals who must manage the reading demands that confront them each day. When was the last time you had instruction in reading? Third grade? Sixth grade? A college study skills course? Yet you spend as much as half of your professional time reading—any other activity that took even 5 percent of your time would have brought you to the seminar room long ago, yet you still use the techniques of childhood. So invest a couple of hours in this chapter—it will pay rich returns in reading efficiency and understanding. And it'll get you through this book more efficiently.

Principles and Techniques of Speed and Power Reading

READ WITH YOUR MIND

Reading happens in the brain, not in the hand, not in the eyes, not on the screen. The eyes serve only to carry information to the mind. The hand turns the pages or clicks the mouse. The screen is just another reading medium, one you adjust to as you adjusted from hard- to paperback books. If you have any doubt about that, watch a blind person read Braille. That's why traditional "speed reading" always fails: it assumes that eye or hand training will improve reading.

---

[9]Mindell, Phyllis, *Power Reading*. New Jersey: Prentice Hall, 1998.

READ PRECISELY AND RIGOROUSLY

Precision reading is a central tenet of power reading. Never try to paraphrase (as you were taught to do in school) early in the reading process. Rather, seek to find what the author says *in the author's own words*. For example, if you wanted to cite the thesis statement, you would copy, flag, or underline rather than paraphrase it. Paraphrasing costs too much time, wastes intellectual energy, and fails to attain the rigor that girds success and leadership.

SCAN AND SKIM FIRST

Use the conventions and structures of writing to increase efficiency and comprehension. Think about your trip to work this morning: you drove on the right side of the street; you stopped at red lights; you signaled for turns. These conventions enabled you to survive. Conventions lie at the heart of all communications; the leader who gets this has taken the first step toward effective communications. You'll see the word *structures* many times in this book, since the reading, writing, speaking, and meeting planning sections all rely on structures. The title page, preface, introduction, thesis statement, paragraph, index, table of contents, and so on offer examples of structures in reading.

Scanning is the rapid search for a particular item. It's the only truly visual reading skill and doesn't engage much brainpower, so you scan very fast, shrinking your in-basket sea to a pool in record time. Scanning defends you against information overload. Whenever someone tells you he reads *The Wall Street Journal* or *The New York Times* every day, you can bet he's scanning the headlines and filtering out all but the relevant articles. As with all the reading skills in this chapter, leadership means you don't have to go it alone, since your community of readers can filter for one another.

Because scanning requires little brainpower, the computer can do most of it for you. Learn and have your staff learn how to use and manage the various search engines, information-seeking, and clipping programs. When scanning works, it winnows the billions of Web bits to bring vital information to your desk or computer.

Skimming, the second rapid reading filter, rewards you when you do it efficiently. Skimming exploits the structures and conventions of written language to speed through any written form. To skim, scroll through or look over the article or book hastily without going into depth. Look for and evaluate the structures that contain vital information: author and title, date of publication, publisher, contents, index, reference list, appendixes. Always look at the beginning (preface, introduction, contents page, date of publication) and end (index, appendixes, notes) structures first. Next, flip the pages from front to back to pick up visual information to judge whether to invest more time. You can skim most books in two minutes or less, covering at least 100,000 words per minute. If the group knows your requirements, others can skim to bring important items to your in-basket. Remember: you don't have to do it alone.

Can you skim digitally? You can, if you scroll the item in question and familiarize yourself with the conventions and structures in the publication. Skimming works best if you can check the end material to judge reference lists and other structures, such as appendixes, glossaries, and indexes. Because there are so many Web sites and they follow such varied organizational patterns, skimming on the computer remains problematic. Still, I predict that Web sites will gradually grow more structured and will develop more universal conventions, making it easier to skim in the future than it is today. Next time you search the Web, think about how you search and read on the screen and how to gain efficiency both on your own and with your community of readers.

Kathleen Barry Albertini, an efficient Web investigator, tracked her application of the power reading filters during a Web search. She varied scanning and skimming to suit the different structures on the Web. She notes, "I use the power reading techniques automatically when I scan long journal articles. While the searching software may highlight the words I requested, I also grab structures such as leads, subtitles, and headings during the skimming phase." But there's a hitch with the very rapid filters. Woody Allen quipped, "I learned to read very fast by running my finger down the middle of the page, and I was able to read *War and Peace* in twenty minutes. It's about Russia." The scanning and skimming filters show what's in a book or Web site but yield virtually no comprehension. The power reader demands understanding, which you gain in the next phase: prereading.

PREREAD

Prereading filters the material that survives scanning and skimming. The reader digs for the structures the writer built into the piece. When prereading, exploit your knowledge of writing conventions to quickly find the central structures: the thesis statement and the topic sentences. When you've finished prereading the piece, you've covered it quickly by *carefully reading only selected portions.* Your skill yields extraordinary understanding because the thesis offers the key to comprehension. Knowing the thesis and the topics enables you to decide whether to read every word deeply and carefully.

Prereading consists of four steps. Simple but not simplistic, the prereading technique speeds you through just about every article, book, study, newspaper, and magazine that crosses your desk, computer screen, e-book, or reading device of the future. But you must adjust it to the material and the medium.

THE FOUR STEPS OF PREREADING

1. **Look at the structure.** For short pieces, step one is merely a quick glance to see the length of the piece and whether the title or subtitle states the thesis. For long articles and whole books, skimming yields a good idea of the structure, order, relevance, and timeliness of the piece. When visiting a new Web site, check the site map or home page to see the structures.

2. **Find the thesis statement.** By convention, modern writers place thesis statements where they're easy to find: in the title or subtitle or near the beginning or end. Always read the beginning few paragraphs (or chapter in a book) and the end few paragraphs (or chapter in a book). In books, the preface or introduction usually state the thesis. If you know the structures of items in your in-basket, they lead you to the places where you're likely to find the thesis quickly. Articles on the Web usually show the thesis in the title or subtitle. Underline, flag, or otherwise mark the thesis if you can: it's the heart of understanding, and you don't want to search for it again later.

3. **Find the topics.** Seek topics only, not details. The writing convention that guides you here is that of the paragraph. The first sentence in the para-

graph usually tells its topic and later sentences flesh out the details. You only want to find and mark (if you can) the paragraph *topics*. In books, the first and/or last paragraphs of the chapters often tell their *topics*. Ignore the details for now.

4. **Decide whether to** *deep read*. At this point, you know a good deal about the piece: its structure, its thesis, and its topics. You also know whether it's well-written, well-organized, and contains information vital to your work. Is it always essential to read every word? No. Our students find that they must deep read only about 10 percent of their in-baskets. Accepting the risk of not reading every word demands courage and confidence in your judgment. Because deep reading represents a huge investment of your limited human capital, use the highest standard to filter for deep reading. If the book or long piece doesn't promise to change your life, decide *not* to deep read it. And manage time by determining whether to deep read now or later.

If reading on the screen, print for deep reading. As of today, it's just too hard to deep read on the screen, with its jiggly letters and poor resolution, not to mention lines that stretch several inches beyond a screen or "pages" that scroll forever. However, clear screens and text-marking devices will soon be readily available for deep reading on the screen. Laura Miller, the Salon.com book critic, notes, "When I find something I can use, I save it . . . and print it out later or keep it on my desktop when I'm writing the article I'm working on." I do the same: I preread the piece on the screen without marking it, then print and file it for later deep reading. Will technological innovation change these practices as it gets easier to mark and store information for easy access? It might, but power readers will be ready because deep reading will always occur in the brain, and computers will never replace the breakfast table, beach, or easy chair.

Once you understand the principles and steps of prereading, tailor the technique to the structures and mediums in your in-basket. For example, if you manage an engineering team, you may choose to preread all the pieces relevant to the specialties on the team, and pass each article on to the person who should deep read it. That keeps you abreast of new developments without bogging you down in details.

The card below shows the results of prereading.

MODEL PREREADING FILE CARD

AUTHOR: Daniel Goleman

TITLE: What Makes a Leader?

PUBLICATION: Harvard Business Review   **DATE:** November-December 1998

PAGE: 93-102

THESIS: "...the most effective leaders are alike in one crucial way: they all have a high degree of what has come to be known as *emotional intelligence*."

TOPICS (list, phrases okay):
Evaluating Emotional Intelligence: determine personal capabilities that drove outstanding performance, asked sr. mgrs to identify most outstanding leaders, dramatic results, emotional intelligence played increasing role at highest levels, other researchers confirmed, persuasive story

Self-Awareness
Self-Regulation
Motivation
Empathy
Social Skill
can be learned

NOTES AND COMMENTS: Excellent piece, worth reading related books. Most of the attributes require advanced communication skills we teach.
Should you deep read? Absolutely.

FLAG AND MARK ANY TEXT YOU MAY LOOK AT LATER

In writing this book, I referred to many references in my library. Among them were books I'd read years ago, valuable books that would prove useful to my readers. I'd marked and flagged some and not others. The marked books yielded quick access to ideas, words to quote, and triggers to my memory. The unmarked books kept their treasures till I reread them (this time I was wise enough to mark and flag).

Marking text fosters comprehension and eases memory. You don't need or want to remember everything you read but you must often go back to find what matters. Unless you possess that rare gift of a photographic memory, you will forget unmarked text, as I did. Indeed, invest time to consider whether your current marking strategies work efficiently for you. Do you still fold page corners, as you did in elementary school? Shed that old-fashioned and damaging habit. Do you still highlight as you did in college? Shun the highlighter—it's a crude tool that lets you carelessly mark whole paragraphs so that when you return to the text you must reread. Reading requires precise thinking and marking strategies. Use little tape flags and a pen; they permit you to select the words and sentences that trigger memory of key information.

After trying a few short pieces, preread this or any other nonfiction book. I recommend Howard Gardner's book *Leading Minds*. In just a few minutes, you'll have superb understanding and the freedom to mine the rich interior details or move on.

DEEP READING AS AN INSTRUMENT OF LEADERSHIP

Once you've decided to invest in deep reading, whether on- or off-screen, attend carefully to every word, every nuance, every idea. Keep a dictionary handy; not a single word should escape you. Have a pencil and a pad of small sticky notes or flags, or the marking function of your program, and mark anything you want to comment on, retain, or use. Mark the items you've always marked: important details, data to recall, notes on the logical flow, and so on. You probably have a shorthand of your own. But go beyond analysis to the higher levels of synthesis and critical reading, which we'll discuss in detail.

SYNTHESIS: THE ULTIMATE LEADERSHIP STRATEGY

Synthesis entails much more than reading: it drives your success as a leader. The definition of *synthesis* is "the combination of separate elements to form a coherent whole" (the word joins the elements, *syn*, meaning together and *tithenai*, meaning to place, so synthesis literally means "putting things together"). The difference between power readers and merely competent ones lies in power readers' ability to create or envision relationships between what they read and what they do at work. Learn synthesis reading because it provokes thought, it works, and it saves time. It makes you not only a more effective reader but a more creative thinker and leader. Indeed, the challenge that awaits you after you finish this book is how you'll synthesize the contents to lead more effectively.

You've preread the book or article and decided to deep read every word. You know the thesis and the topics covered and aim to go beyond, to make it work for you in business. In addition to reading precisely, you're mentally asking, how can I use this information? Synthesis takes you beyond the text. As the poet Helen Vendler wrote, "Through the text the reader becomes a writer, producing new meaning." Synthesis transports you through and beyond the text into your own work life, enabling you to produce new meaning.

Do It Now!

Here are two short paragraphs about leadership. If you're reading for synthesis, you ask questions like these: If it's so easy to miss the signs, how can ordinary people find them? Do I have these three traits? Does my self-regulation make me look like a cold fish, or am I really a cold fish? My competitor, Joe, has that fiery temperament and seems to get all the credit. What can I do about it? Add marginal notes, or *marginalia*, as you read and respond to these paragraphs. Then form the habit of adding marginalia that go beyond the words of the piece.

> The signs of emotional self-regulation, therefore, are not hard to miss: a propensity for reflection and thoughtfulness; comfort with ambiguity and change; and integrity—an ability to say no to impulsive urges.
>
> Like self-awareness, self-regulation often does not get its due. People who can master their emotions are sometimes seen as cold fish—their considered responses are taken as a lack of passion. People with fiery temperaments are frequently thought of as "classic" leaders—their outbursts are considered hallmarks of charisma and power. But when such people make it to the top, their impulsiveness often works against them. In my research, extreme displays of negative emotion have never emerged as a driver of good leadership.[10]

---

[10]Goleman, op. cit.

Avoid passivity. To encourage aggressive reading, deep read provocative pieces that you expect to take issue with. Aggressive reading also tests your language by giving you the chance to hone your resistive and argumentative language in a safe and private environment. Marginalia can't get you fired: aggressive reading acts as your razor-sharp foil of empowerment. Those skills can then transfer into your spoken and written language.

READ LIKE A FENCER: BATTLE WITH THE WRITER

Do It Now!

Read the following extract. Instead of synthesizing, or sympathizing, fence with the author. Use marginalia to parry and thrust, even if you agree. Force yourself to play devil's advocate. Cast your arguments in the grammar of power. If you disagree, tell precisely why. If the author gives spurious arguments, note the error.

In 1990, the rap group 2LiveCrew was prosecuted on obscenity charges (eventually dismissed) for some of the lyrics on its album *As Nasty as They Wanna Be*. A national brouhaha ensued. People who had never heard the music took firm positions. The controversy transformed a moderately successful and by most accounts mediocre album into a phenomenon. It also gave the English language a troubling new phrase. Here are some of its uses in the late 1990s: A blurb for Rosie O'Donnell's television talk show asks us: "Is civility back in style? Or are people (at the top) as nasty as they wanna be?" An article about the campaign tactics of lawyers who want to be judges asks, "Can judicial candidates be as nasty as they wanna be?" The football player Michael Irvin is described by a journalist as wearing "gangsta shades, gold chains and that nasty-as-I-wanna-be smirk." A newspaper story on a Boston neighborhood where many college students live warns that "there are a few nasty-as-they-wanna-be book/video stores." And let us not forget the Internet. The Associated Press has this to say of Internet Explorer 4.0: "Microsoft's Web browser lets computer users be as nasty as they wanna be."

What difference does it make, the reader might ask, whether the lyrics of a song or the name of an album become a cliché? In the first place, the phrase itself reminds us of the source of our crisis, not because of its reference to nastiness, but because it implies that our personalities, no matter how offensive, should be wholly matters of our own choice. . . . Countless messsages in our uncivil era tell us that we have no duties unless we want to have them, even to our own families.[11]

Infiltrate the Enemy Camp: Read What You Abhor

People often choose to deep read a piece because they like it. Consider the opposite option. Deep read books that err, writers with whom you disagree, consultants whose policies threaten your company. Next time you scan the daily paper, seek out the columnists who are wrong on every point. Argue with them. It's a sure way to hone your critical and power reading.

More Reading Suggestions

- Open every meeting with a shared reading. Remember to send copies of articles to everyone before the day of the meeting.

- Form screening groups. An expert in the field reads, marks, and circulates articles—everyone doesn't have to start every piece from scratch.

- Read about leadership.

- If you want to save a newspaper article, find it on the web if available—if not simply clip it.

- Deep read about 10 percent of your in-basket.

- Sponsor a once-a-month brown-bag lunch to discuss a current book or article.

---

[11]Carter, Steven, *Civility: Manners, Morals, and the Etiquette of Democracy.* New York: Basic Books, 1998, pp. 167–8.

Do It Now!

List the structures in any publication on your desk.

Do It Now!

Practice prereading a few times before you move up to deep reading. Try any magazine, editorial, or research piece about any aspect of leadership. You might want to preread one of the books in the reference list for this book. If the periodicals you read are available both electronically and in print, find two pieces of similar length and try prereading one on the screen and the other on hard copy. Compare the amount of time each takes and the outcome. Try filling in a card for each piece, setting it aside, and returning in six months to see whether you retained more from online or from paper reading. If prereading helps, use the same format to record book notes on your word processor.

Do It Now!

Practice each of the four efficiency reading skills on any nonfiction book or journal in your in-basket. When you reach the mentor level, teach your staff the skills.

4

LISTENING LIKE A LEADER

All too often, we enter dialogue with opponents by listening with our mouths, rather than our ears. —STEPHEN CARTER

If reading presents the first receptive language skill, listening combines reception and expression. If your reading skills fall below par, *you* know it; if your listening skills fall below par, *everyone* knows it. If workers could embroider a slogan on the boss's pillow, it would probably be *You're not listening!!!* It's not just what your teenage kids say—it's the biggest complaint when staffs assess leaders. Yes, listening ranks high on every employee's expectation list. Why? One communications expert notes, "The most basic of all human needs is the need to understand and be understood. The best way to understand people is to listen to them." If your listening skills fall short, take heart: you can acquire powerful listening skills without uttering a single word. This chapter opens with an inventory of How Not To's. A high score here is nothing to write home about. A discussion of communication frames, body language, and barriers to listening is followed by specific techniques with examples of when you'd use them and How to Say It lists of response starters.

The dictionary defines *listen* as a verb: "*to make a conscious effort to hear; to attend closely so as to hear.*" Listening is not hearing—it always engages a conscious effort. As you read this book, you *hear* many sounds: the birds singing outside, the hum of the printer, the Mostly Mozart on the radio; but you do not listen to them—you filter them out. Listening is a choice leaders must make. Biographies of great leaders speak of their ability to listen deeply and pay attention. The philosopher Isaiah Berlin commented on John F. Kennedy's ability to turn off everything else and listen intently to one person. Listening holds such a high value that Stephen Carter[12] coined the term *civil listening* and defines it as "listen(ing) to others with knowledge of the possibility that they are right and we are wrong." If you choose to listen when you lead, continue with this chapter.

How Not to Listen

Do It Now!

Score one point for each item you do.

- ❑ Never wait for the speaker to finish the sentence; interrupt
- ❑ Complete the speaker's idea for her
- ❑ Change the subject by bringing it to your own expertise
- ❑ Review Palm Pilot
- ❑ Check pager
- ❑ Think about your next speech
- ❑ Look at the ceiling or floor
- ❑ Look for items in your briefcase
- ❑ Fake attention by nodding your head
- ❑ Always listen the same way
- ❑ Tune out people who look poor or unsuccessful or come from countries you don't like
- ❑ Rest your head on the table
- ❑ Check your watch
- ❑ Read e-mail

---

[12]Carter, *Civility*.

FIVE BARRIERS

1. Filters

We all filter. You may filter people out because of their age, country of origin, race, physical situation, or just because they trigger something that says, "This person isn't worth listening to." It happened to me at a listening seminar. A participant entered. In black leather studded trousers and vest, with a huge key ring at his waist, and tattooed arms, he didn't look like anyone we'd seen at a seminar like this. My reaction was to filter him out. It turned out that he was a splendid human being, intelligent and sensitive, and an excellent course citizen. This humbling experience taught me to listen more carefully to people I tend to filter out.

We also filter people because of their accents. A caller with a strong Southern accent called one day and said, "Mah name is John Doe and Ah'm callin' from London." My first thought was "London, Georgia?" Luckily I waited to hear what he had to say; he actually was calling from London, England, from his executive suite. This Georgia native had earned a promotion each time his company expanded and now was vice president in charge of Europe and the Middle East.

A seminar student met with inappropriate filtering. She suffers from a kind of neurological disorder that affects the speed and quality of her spoken language but does not diminish her ability or competence. She says, "People hear me and decide I'm stupid and not worth listening to."

Can you lead humanely and avoid such negative filtering?

In the leadership chair, you meet people who may differ from you in all the ways listed here. Some are aggressive or hostile. Some speak unintelligible jargon. Some are hard to understand. Some complain all the time. Yet we know that people who are wrong most of the time are sometimes right. Some who are hard to understand may bring great wisdom. Some of those complaints are on target. As a leader you must open yourself to those you might formerly have filtered, especially to them.

The checklist below includes filters people use when they decide not to listen. Check those that block your listening. Jot down the name of a person you've filtered out because he or she has that characteristic. Add other traits that turn you off.

- ☐ Age
- ☐ Sex
- ☐ Race
- ☐ Religion
- ☐ Dress
- ☐ Appearance

- ☐ Voice Quality
- ☐ Accent
- ☐ Ethnicity
- ☐ Animosity
- ☐ Vocabulary
- ☐ Speed

2. Inaccuracy

How often have you been asked to buy Nonna's Italian Bread and bought a white bread? That happens when we listen inaccurately. You get part of the message but miss some of the details. This may prove the most common barrier to listening.

3. Inattention

Let's face it: if you're the boss, you want everyone to listen to you; you don't want to have to listen to others. So you work on the word processor while the salesperson speaks, you spend your listening time planning your next words, you interrupt and never even get the whole message. Senior people tell me they think so much faster than their staffs that they get to the conclusion or implications long before the person stops speaking, which means that they stopped listening as well.

4. Mismatches

Language studies find that mismatches of various kinds interfere with listening comprehension. For example, if the languages of two speakers differ vastly—in their vocabularies, their styles of listening and speaking, or their emotional needs at the moment—they are likely to misunderstand each other. Or their vocabularies. Or their styles of listening and speaking. Or their emotional needs at the moment.

A near-disastrous mismatch occurred when an American company was bought by a European firm. The new leader visited and had a seemingly successful meeting with a group of senior women, assuring them that they would continue to enjoy professional autonomy. Then, as the meeting ended, he said, "Okay, girls, back to the phones."

A mismatched word, understood as a metaphor in one culture but concretely in another, caused international anger and confusion. In the days after 9/11, President Bush spoke of a "crusade" against terror. Americans have long understood crusade in its metaphorical sense: we run crusades in Europe, crusades against poverty, crusades against illnesses, crusades for freedom. But in the Arab Middle East crusade is redolent of what the Crusaders did. This mismatch still dogs us today.

A less serious mismatch occurred during a presentation in the United States when an English executive wanted to erase something. She asked if anyone in the audience had a "rubber."

5. Only One Listening Style

The Janus paradoxes apply to listening as well as to other leadership issues: the leader who always listens the same way will run into trouble sooner or later. Take *empathetic listening*. Research shows that women are more capable of empathetic listening than men. Thus, women who enroll in my seminars rarely mention listening as an issue; they enjoy satisfaction with their listening skills. But empathetic listening rarely is enough in business. It's kind when a mommy says, "Oh, you lost your penny—you must feel so sad" to a three-year-old. But imagine saying, "Oh, you lost ten million this quarter—you must feel so sad," to your boss.

Even the powerful strategy of *precision listening,* in which you take notes on the exact words of the speaker, backfires if someone runs into your office weeping and you pull out your notepad and pencil. Effective listening involves conscious control over several listening techniques.

Communication Frames

Communication entails more than words alone. The actual words transmit only part of the message: how we speak, where we speak, what we wear, whom we address, all influence meanings. These and other elements frame the communication, much as a picture frame borders the images within. Have you ever tried the experiment that asked which of two squares is larger? Depending on the frame, one or the other matching squares looks larger. That shows the power of the frame to shape the message. For this reason, the effective listener attends not only to the words but to the environment in which they are uttered. For example, "You look great!" can be meant as harassment in certain work situations or as a commentary on health in others. Later, in the chapters on speaking and meetings, we'll revisit the notion of frames. Now that we have explored elements of listening, let's look at ways to grow your listening ability.

LEARN TO LISTEN

Paradoxically, you first "listen" with the eyes—you attend to body language and whether it matches the words. As much as two thirds of the message in face-to-face communication may come from nonverbal cues, which can complement the spoken words or bear the true message. That's why phone conferences pose such problems—you get no visual cues. Still, although most people report themselves to be good readers of body language and faces, studies show they are not. "Listening" to body language lies at the core of empathy, of leadership, of power. Reading body language meets more complexity in the diverse workplace. The rules of nonverbal communication vary widely from one culture to another, making it especially difficult to listen to those with different backgrounds from yours. For example, American culture is a no-touch, distant culture, while Mediterranean culture is high-touch. At a party, you may find yourself backing away from the high-touch Frenchman and trying to get closer to the no-touch German. In that sense, different cultures "speak" different nonverbal languages. You as a leader must learn those languages if you wish to listen effectively.

Listening also requires obedience to the rules of body language. You may have learned gestures that not only suggest you're not listening but actually block your ability to listen. On the list on page 38, check listeners' body language that pleases you; then check the items that you do. Do you demonstrate the pleasing or the hostile body language of listening?

Do It Now!

In the first column, check Pleasing or Displeasing—in the second column, check the behaviors that you display when listening. If uncertain, either ask others to do the checklist on you or have yourself tape-recorded.

Although body language can prove ambiguous and hard to read, we find wide agreement on the signals that say, "I'm listening" versus those that say, "I'm not listening." Positive listening poses don't just show respect to the speaker; they also help you concentrate on the message. The leader who opens his body, makes eye contact, and keeps notes doesn't just look as though he's listening—he's probably really listening.

LISTEN SILENTLY

In later sections, you'll find sentence starters and words to say to apply various listening techniques, but remember that talking doesn't take place during listening: it's a silent activity. So what can you do to ensure appropriate listening behaviors?

SEVEN SILENT WAYS TO FOSTER LISTENING

1. **Ensure visibility.** It's easier to listen if you see the speaker's eyes and gestures; choose a spot that enables you to do so.

2. **Open the body.** The open body is a power gesture, one that must enter your repertoire if you wish to gain authority as a leader. Everything is as open as it can be—the shoulders open, the eyes make contact, the arms open on the chair arms, the fists are open (unless you're taking notes).

3. **Show you're awake.** Admittedly, some people at certain times may close their eyes and drop their chins in order to listen carefully. But if you do it often, you're seen as hostile, negative, uninterested. Keep the head up, facing the speaker.

	PLEASING	DISPLEASING	I DO
Lays head on table			
Closes eyes			
Dozes			
Holds pencil and appears to take notes			
Whispers or writes notes to others			
Gazes at the wall or ceiling			
Makes eye contact with speaker			
Slams pencil down and crosses arms			
Glares at speaker			
Works on something other than current topic			
Smiles and nods in agreement or looks uncertain			
Doodles			
Taps toe on floor			
Kicks crossed leg up and down			
Slouches			
Sits up with head high and palms open			
Chews gum			
Uses cell phone			
Walks around the room			
Walks out during presentation			
Looks at watch			

4. Connect with speaker's eyes. Eye contact holds the secret to all communication. When you give the gift of frequent eye contact (not staring!), you give the gift of attention to the speaker and the gifts of concentration and focus to yourself. Eye contact plays a vital role in speaking as well, as you'll see later.

5. Gesture to show attention. Nod, smile, frown, shake your head. Responsive gestures both force you to listen and show that you're listening.

6. Keep a notebook handy. When an encounter begins, you may not yet know whether notes will be required, but be prepared.

7. Take precise notes when appropriate. If the stories and vignettes in this book sound real, it's because they are. When I travel the world, my notepads travel with me. Whenever a useful or interesting story comes up, it appears on the notepad. Before you know it, enough true stories have accumulated to write a book. The simple act of keeping precise notes focuses attention and spurs memory.

Thus, although you remain silent (even if you're the CEO!), the quality of the nonverbal behavior shapes the quality of the listening. In addition, specific techniques and replies can advance conversations and meetings.

Listen Responsively

Listening Precisely
In the last chapter, you met the notion of precise reading, in which you do not seek to paraphrase but instead understand the text in the writer's own words. The idea of precise reading gave birth to the idea of *precise listening*, in which you take notes using as many of the exact words of the speaker as possible (you can't write fast enough to note all the words). This simple technique offers huge benefits to those who seek to lead by preventing filtering, assuring accuracy, lessening conflict, reducing the memory burden, yielding a permanent record, focusing attention, aiding in persuasion, and clarifying directions.

But, perhaps most vital for the leader, precise listening assures speakers that you care what they say.

Our leadership seminars feature a listening experiment that you can easily duplicate in your office. Participants present brief self-introductions. Listeners are instructed to pay close attention to half the speakers and to listen *precisely* to the other half. They are asked to record as many of the exact words as possible. After setting the notes aside for two days, they retell what they remember. The results astound. When they take notes, people retain both the content of the recorded messages and the flavor of each individual's language. Listening carefully without precise notes results in generalizations, few or wrong details, and few exact words. After they see the stunning differences, everyone resolves to take precise notes in the future.

Do It Now!

Do your first piece of action research. Set up a precise listening experiment like the one above. The content can include self-introductions, oral reading, conversations with staff members, or any other material you wish to retain. Take precise notes half the time; pay close attention half the time. Wait a couple of hours or days and see what you remember of each.

Repeat or Paraphrase

To be sure you got the message straight, repeat the exact words or paraphrase. Repetition clarifies, shows that you're paying attention, and lets you rehearse the message to help you remember it. Hearing his own words may also remind the speaker to speak more clearly. To avoid distortion, favor precise repetition of at least the key words—the verbs and nouns. Paraphrasing can help if the message is cast in unfamiliar language, is especially inarticulate, or is offensive and not repeatable. Here is your first How to Say It of sentence starters when you seek to repeat or paraphrase.

Repetition and Paraphrase Sentence Starters

Repetition	*Let me repeat exactly what you said . . .*
	This will help me serve you better. You said . . .
	You seem to have said . . .
Paraphrase	*If I understand you correctly . . .*
	You seem to be saying . . .
	My interpretation is . . .
	So you mean . . .

Empathize

Empathy means "identification with and understanding of another's situation." The empathetic listener doesn't judge, advise, or instruct, but reflects sympathetically on what the person said and to the body language. Empathetic listening has its roots in psychoanalysis and focuses on the feelings of the speaker. In the executive suite, there are moments when empathetic listening works: when someone sits weeping before you, when you must deliver bad news, when you must let someone go. We often work with people who have been laid off in downsizing. Their anger is not only at the layoff but at the insensitive way it takes place. Leadership doesn't mean delivering only good news but it does mean showing compassion during difficult times. Empathetic listening helps you do so. It also avoids what Stephen Carter calls *confrontational listening*: "not listening at all; it is not respectful and leads to no dialogue."[13]

Words That Empathize

Oh, my.

That must have upset you.

You seem distressed (sad, annoyed, angry). (Avoid, "I know how you feel." It insults and it's not true.)

What a frustration.

---

[13]Carter, *Civility.*

Clarify

Clarify when you're not sure you understand. Clarification questions go beyond repetition. They seek expansion.

Words That Seek Clarification

Please explain . . .

What does xxx mean?

Please clarify the concept of the flat corporation.

This use of the term xxx needs explanation.

Probe

Probe for additional information. The best probe questions seek specific, open-ended information. Probes direct the questions without suggesting the answers.

Words That Probe

Please give me the details.

What exactly happened?

What happened next?

What was the problem?

When . . .

Who . . .

Where . . .

Do It Now!

Next to each of the barriers listed on the following chart, note a situation in which your listening suffered as a result.

BARRIERS THAT IMPEDE LISTENING	HOW LISTENING SUFFERED
Filters	
Inaccuracy	
Inattention	
Mismatches	
One Style	

Do It Now!

Think of a situation in which your listening skills failed. Write a short narrative of what happened. Next, using the information in this chapter, note what aspect went wrong. Did you filter inappropriately, suffer a mismatch, misread the frame? Such failure and success analyses yield insights that guide future action.

Do It Now!

You'll find below a list of listening situations typical of those faced by leaders. Next to each, write the listening techniques you'd apply, note the body language you'd use, and write the spoken response that might prove most appropriate.

Situation 1

At a team meeting, an angry speaker says, "Whenever my group suggests an approach, the rest of the team shoots it down. You don't seem to feel we play an important role in this business."

Listening stance:

_____

_____

Listening technique and verbal response:

_____

_____

Situation 2

A hostile employee sneers, "Do me a favor, will you? When the big boys are playing, you stay off the field."

Listening stance:

_____

_____

Listening technique and verbal response:

_____

_____

Situation 3

An employee starts weeping during a difficult evaluation.

Listening stance:

_____

_____

Listening technique and verbal response:

_____

_____

Situation 4

The engineers are presenting. They show an incomprehensible slide and say something like: "You can enable an additional set of result codes using the W command to report progress of the negotiation phase of error-correction mode. These codes report the carrier slipped and the error-correction protocol . . ."

Listening stance:

_____

_____

Listening technique and verbal response:

_____

_____

Situation 5

You are presenting information to the public. A seemingly crazed audience member stands, dominates the floor, and rambles on about how the Masons have taken over the factory and will destroy it.

Listening stance:

_____

_____

Listening technique and verbal response:

_____

_____

In sum, although listening is a silent activity, your listening responses can advance the conversation and reinforce your leadership stature. It's no wonder Glenn Rifkin wrote in *The New York Times* of a world leader, "Her most notable quality, colleagues say, is her ability to listen and process what she hears.

5

LEADING WITHOUT WORDS: PRESENCE, CHARISMA, AND NONVERBAL COMMUNICATIONS

We respond to gestures with extreme alertness and . . . in accordance with an elaborate and secret code that is written nowhere, known by none, and understood by all. —EDWARD SAPIR

The executive suite stretches your ability to receive language through reading, listening, and observing. But it's the language you *generate* that serves as the crucible of leadership—and the first form of expressive language is the one without voice: your presence. Leadership presence refers to all the nonverbal aspects of expression: style, posture, body language, eye contact, gesture, touch, and silence. This chapter tells how small changes in these elements can spur big changes in leadership presence.

Style

My files overflow with style stories: some funny, some sad, some dramatic. But they all end happily. Of all the changes that can foster successful leadership, style proves the easiest and most fun. We have little systematic research to guide us here, so use experience and common sense as you ponder your clothing style as part of leadership presence.

One day a consultant attended a meeting with a senior executive and a subordinate selected for fast-track promotion. He'd never met either of the gentlemen. A seat at the end of a hallway gave him the benefit of a long view as they walked together. Both men looked good enough; still, the consultant knew who was the senior and who the junior on the basis of clothing alone: the senior wore well-cut, well-fitted clothing in good fabrics, while the junior wore the opposite. The differences didn't just reflect different salary levels. One of these men knew he had to look like a leader; the other did not.

Another story holds more drama. A young woman stopped me after a communications seminar to tell me that she faced a layoff and to seek help. She said she aimed to go into marketing. One look at her said that no one would buy from her. She wore a stained cotton calico dress (she also slouched) and a hairdo that went out of style before she was born. Fortunately for her, her potential had been noted and her manager had budgeted money for learning experiences for her. She took a seminar that included a style component and seemed to get the ideas. Three years later, her name appeared on a leadership course roster. When she strode into the room beautifully groomed, tastefully (but not expensively) dressed in a clean light-colored blazer over a black skirt and sweater, one could see both her willowy figure and her use of what she'd learned about style. She was well on her way to a senior leadership position. Style is not rocket science—anyone can learn how to put him- or herself together.

Is it possible to dress too well? It sure is. A new executive at an upstate New York firm called to say that people told her she was intimidating and asked for my help. We arranged to meet a week later, on casual day, it turned out. This beautiful woman wore a cashmere sweater and suede pants with one designer piece of jewelry—impeccable, stunning, and wrong for the setting. Discussion revealed that she bought her clothes in Paris. That might work in New York City or San Francisco, but definitely not in Rochester, New York. She learned to moderate her style (among other changes) to make herself less intimidating and gradually gained acceptance. What matters is not only that you dress well but that you dress appropriately for the setting and the audience.

Another sad story in my files occurred at a weekend conference of an ethnic group whose members take great pride in their appearance. The conference participants wore suits, ties, chic shoes, clothing that bespoke pride in their professional accomplishments. Unfortunately the CEO hadn't thought about the group whose conference she addressed; she decided that one dresses down on Saturdays. So she stood at the podium in a sweater and the kind of pants that get terribly rumpled when you're sitting on an airplane. She dressed far less well than those whom she sought to lead. It sapped her authority and credibility with this audience.

Yes, style matters. The best engineers in the skunk works can wear anything they please but they must consider style when moving into management. Sure, Einstein didn't have to think about style. But you're not Einstein. We're way beyond the rigid "dress for success" days, but nobody wants to follow a slob. And there's no one formula for style: industry, region, ethnic background, and other influences predict what will work in various situations. The ideas that follow will help you avoid the worst mistakes; if they look like Greek to you, go to the best shop in town or have the firm hire a stylist for you.

TEN STYLE ESSENTIALS

1. Have your style evaluated by an image consultant.

2. Make your hair transparent. It should blend with overall appearance.

3. Follow the jewelry rule: less is more.

4. Don't let business casual slip into business sloppy.

5. Be meticulous about cleanliness.

6. Dress for the role.

7. Respect your ethnicity.

8. Avoid odors. If you wear scent restrict yourself to one—more people than you think are allergic or find any odor offensive.

9. Remember Goldilocks. Style shouldn't be too big or too small—it should be just right!

10. Invest in a few classic garments.

The Nonverbal Language of Leadership

He holds a high position in an international company. He rose through technical ability. He stood before an executive presentation seminar class, arms at his sides, gazing at the ceiling, and said, "I'm a boring speaker." And he did indeed bore, in large part because of his stiffness—you wouldn't buy a used car from this guy, let alone budget the fifteen million dollars he requested. Could he learn the nonverbal language of leadership? He sure did.

Edward Sapir said, "We respond to gestures with extreme alertness and . . . in accordance with an elaborate and secret code that is written nowhere, known by none, and understood by all." That secret code extends to the executive suite: your power, charisma, and credibility rest on understanding and expressing that code. For example, a study of charisma finds that "Those who were charismatic were simply more animated than others. They smiled more, spoke faster, pronounced words more clearly, and moved their heads and bodies more often. They were also more likely to touch others during greetings. What we call charisma can better be understood as human expressiveness."[14]

Do It Now!

A great way to see whether you exude charisma involves turning the sound off and carefully watching a video of a meeting or presentation. With no sound, the message emerges vividly.

Silent videotapes reveal whether the presentation or meeting succeeded and whether the speaker moved like a leader. One tape in my collection shows the speaker playing with a pen, another shows a speaker whose hands repeatedly poke in and out of his pockets, and another has a speaker who looks at the ceiling through most of the talk. Another shows a speaker who winces every time a mistake occurs; another has a speaker who says just the right words as

---

[14]Kouzes, James M. and Barry Z. Posner, *The Leadership Challenge.* San Francisco: Jossey-Bass, 1987, p. 24.

she turns her back to the audience to speak to a slide. Thus, silent video proves an inexpensive and effective learning tool.

FIFTEEN PRINCIPLES OF NONVERBAL LEADERSHIP

What if you not only lack charisma but don't think you can ever acquire it? In other words, can you succeed without charisma? Some successful CEOs lack and probably will never have charisma. Their strategic decisions alone bring them followers. It's okay if you never attain charisma; it's worth trying but don't take yourself off the leadership track just because you lack it.

Allowing for individual variations, we can generalize about gestures and other nonverbal aspects of leadership. Remember those Janus paradoxes, however: if you're the one in power you have more freedom to violate the principles set out below. And for every principle outlined here, you'll probably think of instances in which someone successfully violated it. Remember also that all behavior should reflect the environment in which it occurs: what you do at a gym differs from what you do at a keynote speech.

1. It's Not About You.

First, weigh the nonverbal implications of the principle "It's not about you." Just as you don't talk about yourself, you don't gesture about (or to) yourself. The more you attend to the audience and content, the more confident and relaxed you appear; the more you worry about yourself, the less confident you appear. It's the self-conscious or inattentive executive who conveys a message of uncertainty, snobbery, apathy, or aggression.

Research also shows that the leader's behavior shapes the behavior of others: if the leader looks at the speaker, nods, makes eye contact, and seems interested, the speaker tends to show more appropriate behavior.

2. Open the Body.

Here's a great general principle that applies at nearly all times in nearly all situations. Research on gestures and nonverbal presentations shows that the open, relaxed body conveys power while the closed, rigid body conveys weakness. Your mother was right: hold the head high, smile, open the arms, the elbows, and the palms.

3. Touch with Your Eyes.

Research shows that "increased eye contact results in perceptions of dynamism, dominance, believability, and persuasiveness . . ." while those who "averted their gaze were perceived as less credible."[15] Eye contact is perhaps the most important gesture in the repertoire. In informal conversation, frequent eye contact offers a way to link yourself to others, to gain charisma, to look into their souls. To help define eye contact, let's dissect the word *contact*. It comprises two parts: *con* means together, *tact* comes from *tangere* meaning "to touch." So eye contact literally means to touch with the eyes, not to skim, not scan but to look long enough to touch. In one-to-one conversation, spend about half the time touching the eyes of your partner; in presentations, touch the eyes of people in various parts of the room; in speeches to very large audiences, look for the eyes even when you can't actually touch them. Eye contact matters so much that this rule prevails: **Say every word to a person, with eye contact.** It doesn't mean staring—by all means don't hold and never let go (that can be seen as aggressive or hostile), but look at the person when you speak. This rule applies to both formal and informal conversations and all speeches and presentations in the United States. The rules differ in other countries—check when traveling abroad.

4. Sit Like a Leader.

Look at underlings: they slouch, they squirm, they play with their pencils, they clasp their elbows, their knees pop up and down, their legs splay. Now look at a leader you admire: he sits straight, her arms rest comfortably on the arms or back of the chair, his head remains high, her feet remain relaxed yet ready. Above all, the leader reflects dignity—and the body language expresses it.

Research tells us forward-leaning toward a conversational partner, combined with increased eye contact, reflects the desire to be liked. If you wish to be liked as a leader, and not everyone does, try these gestures.

---

[15] Judee K. Burgoon, David B. Buller, and W. Gill Woodall, *Nonverbal Communications: The Unspoken Dialogue.* New York: McGraw Hill, 1996, p. 383.

5. Hold the Head High.

The head gets most attention: change the way you hold your head and you change your image. There are several characteristically weak head positions and gestures but the most common is chin down with eyes downcast or furtively glancing upward, a modest gesture of subservience that won't work for leaders. The expressive face gives the impression that you are more friendly, of better character than the poker face. Speakers who nod, smile, and avoid distracting gestures and facial expressions have a greater chance to influence others.

6. Smile.

Roger Axtell, in *Gestures: The Do's and Taboos of Body Language Around the World*,[16] asserts that the smile is the "ultimate gesture": it is absolutely universal and rarely misunderstood. But some of us have been taught that one must be grim to be serious—that's simply wrong. One of my students learned the value of the smile from his grandson. Although a pleasant man, he rarely smiled at business meetings or presentations. He was videotaped at a public speaking seminar and showed his grandchild the tape. The child said, "Grandpa, you look mad." That spurred him to add smiles to his nonverbal repertoire. When appropriate, the smile gives credibility, shows confidence, and makes for a pleasant experience. And remember what I call the "dental society" smile, with teeth showing. It should, of course, look natural and not forced.

7. Coordinate Gestures and Words.

Scholars call this congruence. When the words and gestures complement one another, the message gets across clearly. In contrast, when the words say one thing and the gestures say another, neither message gets across. Think of the executive who says, "We're optimistic about the coming quarter" while wringing his hands. When the gestures mirror the words, both the words and the body carry the message.

---

[16]Axtell, Roger, *Gestures: The Do's and Taboos of Body Language Around the World*. New York: Wiley, 1998.

8. Show Sincerity.

"Always be sincere whether you mean it or not." These funny words uttered by Flanders and Swann, English comedians of several decades ago, tell a basic truth. People believe those who seem sincere. We've already highlighted the elements of sincerity: eye contact, attentiveness, open body, response to conversational partners. Experience has shown that those who avoid bluster, carry themselves without pretension, and do the gestures cited here are seen as more sincere than those who do not. Still, keep the Janus paradoxes in mind: Muhammad Ali blustered and was immodest yet he gained millions of followers with his moxie and outrageous style.

9. Maintain Control.

The word control appears often in this book. Control your words, your appearance, and your body if you wish to lead and persuade others. Weak speakers show loss of control. They flail arms, they add unnecessary gestures (scratching the nose, jingling coins, playing with hair, and so on), they sway, they pace. If you want to look poised, control your movements. If you want to express passion through large gestures, control matters even more.

10. Reach Out and Touch Someone.

We touch with the eyes, but real touch also establishes relationships. The touching must be brief, not intimate, and appropriate to the setting (shaking hands rather than hugging in most business settings, a light touch on the arm while shaking hands).

11. Influence Through Nonverbal Communications.

"Speakers attempting to be persuasive (1) make more eye contact with their listeners, (2) gesture more, (3) use more affirmative nods, (4) are more facially expressive, (5) engage in less self-manipulation, and (6) lean backward less."[17] They also adopt closer distances to the audience and are moderately relaxed.

---

[17]Burgoon, op. cit., p. 401.

12. Select Suitable Trappings.

We hear of the trappings of power: the big house, the fancy car, the crown, the scepter, the expensive suit, the fine jewelry. You're more likely to be accepted as a leader if you select the trappings that match the way you want to lead. Your trappings may include a gavel, a fine watch, designer clothing, a lapel flag, a breast cancer ribbon, khaki pants, designer ties or scarves, or particular pieces of jewelry.

13. Model the Behaviors You Want to See in Others.

Research shows that adults adopt behaviors they see modeled. You want openness? You want warm handshakes? You want courteous body language? You're the boss—model them and see everyone do the same.

14. Foster or Discourage Through Nonverbal Communications.

Change the actions of those with whom you work (as well as of customers and salespeople) by using positive or negative gestures and eye contact. When someone is presenting, try nodding, smiling, looking confused if the message isn't clear, taking notes, touching a shoulder at the end, and, of course, applauding superb work. In the same way, use negative gestures to reveal displeasure. For example, narrow the eyes, stare, scowl, make a fist, cross the arms, or avert the eyes to show displeasure at what you see. Once in a while, keep your reactions secret with a poker face.

15. Value Silence.

Good speakers know it; good leaders know it; good listeners know it. Silence empowers you, augments your message, allows others time to speak. Build strategic silence into every talk, every major speech, every meeting. Review audiotapes to ascertain whether you rush from one word to another or pause to stress points. Review meeting videos to check whether you use your power to give voice to the silent ones: the quiet, the shy, and the weak.

Off the Desk Chair and on to the Podium

As you attain higher and more visible positions, you'll be asked to speak more often and to larger and more varied audiences. And when addressing these audiences, you stand not as Joe Doe, but as Company X. If Joe Doe moves like an underling, Company X looks like an underling; if Joe Doe moves with confidence and candor, Company X looks strong and honest. To represent your company or industry effectively, build a repertoire of presentation and speech gestures and grow them as the audiences grow. If you gesture naturally, you may only have to refine and control what you already do. If you're a stiff speaker, add one or two gestures each time you speak. In *Body Politics*[18] Nancy Henley notes, "Nonverbal gestures carry the most influence when they are natural and not affected, when they enhance and harmonize with the verbal message." To be sure that your new gestures carry influence, practice them enough so that they are natural and not affected. Ideas in this section come from the film director Ron Mix and my own coach, the actress Vicki Casarett.

A DOZEN PODIUM GESTURES

   1. Rest well. The director Ron Mix coined the useful term *resting position*. Most of your speaking time is not spent in gesture—it is spent at rest. Adopt a comfortable resting position and hold it when you're not gesturing. If you have a podium, your arms can rest comfortably on it. If you're standing near a computer, one arm can rest on it. Or one hand can rest in your pocket. Whatever you choose, the resting position should look comfortable and relaxed.

   2. Lay a strong foundation with the feet. The traditional power stance holds the feet about a foot apart, facing forward. Avoid crossing the ankles, bouncing, or holding one leg up. If you tend to sway, your legs probably lack a strong foundation. It helps to wear comfortable shoes.

---

[18]Henley, Nancy M., *Body Politics*. New York: Simon & Schuster, 1977.

3. **Face the audience.** If using visuals, place them where you can glance at them; then face the audience to speak. If using a pointer, stand next to the visual so you don't have to turn away.

4. **Open the arms.** If the video shows that your elbows stay close to the body when the arms gesture, learn to lift the elbows—one of my students describes it as "airing the armpits."

5. **Copy Olympians: lift both arms over the head in a gesture of triumph.** A newspaper photo montage of Olympic winners shows every one holding arms up in this victorious gesture. Beware, however, that this gesture carries great drama—it'll look silly if you're asking the time.

6. **Show growth by lifting and separating the arms.** Show shrinkage by starting the arms open and closing them smoothly or dropping them.

7. **Limn parallel ideas with parallel gestures.** The sweep from one side to the other, the chop from top to bottom or side to side.

8. **Point with the open palm rather than the finger (finger pointing reminds people of shooting and usually appears hostile).**

9. **Walk toward and away from the audience.** For example, if addressing a particular audience member, walk toward her and then return to the podium.

10. **Create new gestures by observing successful speakers and copying theirs (or get a great speech coach).**

11. **Avoid the worst gestures: banging fist on table; using finger as pointer; turning back to listeners; hugging or shrugging the shoulders; standing with legs wide and fists at waist; looking at watch; playing with glasses, hair, pockets, pen, etc.**

12. **Build silence into talks.**

As you gain ease and confidence, make a point to expand your repertoire. A professional speaker tells this story of expansion and growth. Last year, she had to deliver a major conference presentation to an audience of twelve hundred. It was one of those conferences that offered five keynotes and several sessions; the audience members might be burned out by the time they arrived. So the speaker decided to attempt a funny beginning. With Vicki Casarett's guidance, she learned a number of new and difficult gestures: they had to portray lack of confidence, anxiety, and inadequacy. First, the host of the session agreed to collaborate by acting shocked while he gave the introduction. The speaker sat on a chair on the speaker's platform, legs splayed and feet pigeon-toed, knees bent inward, arms clutched and unclutched. She played with a pen, looked at the ceiling, adjusted a shoulder pad, and repeatedly straightened her notecards. The audience got the message and greeted the comedy with sustained laughter—a challenging but successful way to start a speech. And powerful proof of the value of gestures and of silence.

Do It Now!

Ask five colleagues to evaluate your style at work or engage an image consultant to visit your closet.

Videotape yourself as you walk through a talk with gestures only, no words. Next, try the gestures listed above. Evaluate them. Add one new gesture each time you speak. Have your next presentation videotaped. As you view it without sound, list the gestures you made and assess their level. If your gestures don't appear on this list, give them names to help you remember the ones that worked.

All in all, nonverbal communications yield an efficient and effective way to establish your authority and model appropriate behaviors for others. Here's looking at you, baby!

But looking great is not enough. You must speak like a leader as well.

6

TALKING LIKE A LEADER

If you can't explain an idea or a policy plainly in one or two sentences, it's not yours; and if it's not yours, no one you speak to will be persuaded of it, or . . . know what you are. —STANLEY FISH

The nonverbal aspects of leadership create and reinforce the overall impression. But the ability to lead ultimately rests on the ability to speak. This chapter exposes the kinds of sentences and words that sap authority and proposes the kinds of sentences and words that gain authority. Note, however, that this chapter is not just about sentences—it's about how our utterances reflect and shape leadership, how we can actually change our way of interacting with the world through small and easy changes in language. Believe me, it's much simpler to alter speech patterns than to alter the inner soul: we've watched thousands of people transform themselves by transforming their language.

Grammar that Saps Authority

"I" STATEMENTS

Before we begin, look at the quotations below and check the sentences you speak.

- ❑ *I disagree with you.*
- ❑ *You're wrong.*

❑ *I like that idea.*

❑ *I expect you to get that in on time.*

❑ *I'm pleased with your job performance.*

❑ *I will lead the company to success.*

❑ *I will not yield, I will not relent, I will not rest . . .*

You may wonder, "What's wrong with those sentences? I say them all the time." Good—read this chapter. Although grammatically correct, each of these sentences offers up a weak or other negative language form by forgetting to ask the first question you met earlier, "What is it *not* about?" Let's look at the statements above to see what's wrong with them and how to transform them by asking the three questions: "What is it not about?" "What is it about?" "What does it do?"

I disagree with you. You're wrong. These two sentences err in making personal that which should remain professional. Both come on like gangbusters and put the conversation partner on the defensive. Let's see how the three questions limn what's wrong and transform these sentences.

I disagree with you. First, what is it not about? It's not about you, even if it seems so. Second, what is it about? Ah, now we see the profound flaw in this statement. It isn't about anything. We have to imagine what you disagree about; perhaps it's the engineering proposal the other guy touts. The transformed sentence begins, *The (your) engineering proposal . . .*

Finally, what does it do? *The engineering proposal fails to meet our specifications.* At last, we know what the sentence meant to say. The transformed statement still disagrees but has blunted its overt hostility and actually says something you can argue about, without rancor, without hostility, without personal attack. Let's look at the next statement: *You're wrong*. These words almost invariably are perceived as hostile and personal. First, what is it not about? It's not about "you." What is it about? It's about something missing, perhaps a legal interpretation. So the sentence now begins, *Your (or that) legal interpretation . . .* Third, what does it do? *Your legal interpretation has no precedent.* The transformed statement has replaced vagueness and a hostile stance with content and a neutral stance.

I like that idea. By now it should be easy to figure out why this seemingly kind statement actually abdicates leadership. Try this one yourself.

I expect you to get that in on time. This weak sentence suggests that it's all about you. But ask the first question, what is it not about? And you realize that it's not about you. Ask the second question, what is it about (or, in grammar terms, what is the subject)? Well, what did you mean to talk about? That job? Sounds like "that job" answers the second question. Now ask the third question, what does it do? The sentence now says, *That job must arrive on time*, or *That job must get to my desk by Tuesday.* Now you're delivering a clear direction focusing on what you really intended to say.

I'm pleased with your job performance. This one sounds fine. How can we transform it to a leadership statement? Once more, what is it not about? You didn't really mean to make yourself the subject of this sentence. What is it about? Your job performance. What does it do? *Your job performance has speeded the invoice process* (and add "thank you" if appropriate).

Now compare the first and the transformed sentence: *I'm pleased with your job performance. Your job performance speeded the invoice process. Thanks.*

My files contain a letter written by a competent scientist, a Ph.D., expressing concern about an issue. The person wondered why the recommendations got no respect. The short letter is plagued by these "I" statements: *I've recently heard . . . ; . . . which I'm hoping . . . ; I'm dismayed that . . . ; for I am certain; I have brought this up in conversation; I can assure you that . . . ; I once; I emphasize . . . ; I have heard a reaction; If I imagine; I would not be able to; I urge you to; I am absolutely certain; I fail to understand; I would rather see; I exhort you.* Any one of these "I" statements does little harm by itself, but the accumulation drains the letter of its power and persuasiveness.

The last sentences, *I will lead the company to success*, and *I will not yield, I will not relent, I will not rest . . .* , evoke an added issue about leaders' language in business and in politics. Some annoying campaigners haven't figured out the harm "I" statements do. Those who keep talking about themselves show their lack of interest in those they lead and suggest a high level of self-involvement.

Worse, Renana Brooks[19] asserts that they seek to use language to dominate others and force them into victimhood. She describes a "dependency-creating language . . . of contempt and intimidation to shame others into submission and desperate admiration." She cites "several dominating linguistic techniques to induce surrender. . . ." They include what she calls "personalization . . . localizing the attention of the listener on the speaker's personality . . . as the only person capable of producing results." Thus, "I" statements exemplify a Janus paradox: they can both weaken the speaker and dominate others.

Finally, consider the "I" statement used in Martin Luther King, Jr.'s great speech uttered on the steps of the Lincoln Memorial in 1962. Each paragraph opens with, "I have a dream . . ." but if you read or view the speech on tape, you'll hear that "I" stands symbolically for all mankind—that speech is not about Dr. King!

Does this mean you'll never say "I" again? Of course not. If your leadership style seeks domination and suppression of others, you'll utter many "I" statements. If you lack leadership style or confidence, you'll utter many "I" statements. If you want to seem friendly and approachable, you'll utter many "I" statements in the mistaken belief that they work. But if you aim to lead powerfully and humanely; if you aim to foster autonomy; if you aim to empower others, shun most "I" statements. Except when you mean to talk about yourself. A story sometimes illustrates a point or reflects a common humanity—in those situations "I" statements yield authority and clarity.

Read any great political speech and you'll find few or no "I" statements: *The Gettysburg Address* has none, the best inauguration and business speeches have few. Tony Blair's brilliant speech[20] before the American Congress on July 18th, 2003, had nearly 3500 words: "I" appeared less than 1/2 of 1 percent of the time.

---

[19]Brooks, Renana, "A Nation of Victims," *The Nation,* June 30, 2003 (http://thenation.com/docprint.mhtml?i=2003630&s=brooks)

[20]Blair, Tony, "A Fight for Liberty," *Wall Street Journal,* July 18, 2003 (http://www.opinionjournal.com/forms/printThis.html?id=110003758)

Do It Now!

Search the Web for a political or executive speech. Count the number of "I" statements. If you have a transcript of one of your speeches, count the number of "I" statements (my students find 10 percent or more in their first seminar talks).

Audiotape a small meeting and have your words transcribed. Count the "I" statements. Too many? Dominating? Weak? Appropriate?

As you gain control of language, gain control of "I" statements.

PRONOUNS: NOT ALL EQUAL

"I" isn't the only pronoun. A pronoun takes the place of a noun: for example *I, you, we, they, us*. We give little thought to pronouns, yet they carry much weight in a sentence. All pronouns are not equal. "I" usually fails. "You" is problematic; it works brilliantly in statements such as, "You represent the future leadership of our company;" but it fails in "You people are always ruining projects." The Blair speech contains phrases like these: "And you have an extraordinary record . . . ," "And our job," ". . . my nation that watched you grow, that you fought alongside and now fights alongside you. . . ."

A notorious "you" failure occurred during a recent presidential campaign. A candidate speaking to the NAACP used the term "you people" several times. In the furor that followed, no one remembered his economic message—only his unfortunate "you people." He soon dropped out of the race. Don't let that happen to you.

But the pronoun that always works is "we." Researchers who recorded team meetings and analyzed the language found that teams that used "we" more than "I" and "you" worked together more successfully. The writers noted, "The way team members talk to one another indicates the extent to which they feel interdependent."[21]

---

[22]Donnellon, Anne, *Team Talk: The Power of Language in Team Dynamics*. Boston: Harvard Business School Press, 1996.

The value of "we" can't be overemphasized. The executive who uses "we" to refer to the team, group, or company increases the chance that his leadership will be acknowledged. Look at this excerpt from the radio speech Winston Churchill gave just as the Germans were about to invade England during World War II: "We shall go on to the end, we shall fight in France, we shall fight on the seas and the oceans, we shall fight with growing confidence and growing strength in the air. . . ." Was Churchill planning to fight? Absolutely not—he sat safe in his bunker, but he was wise enough to know that few would follow if he said, "You people shall fight." The Blair speech contains more than twice as many "we" as "I" statements; for example, "We are bound together as never before. . . . If we are wrong. . . . We will have . . . We will deliver it. . . ." So be wise enough to use "we" when you aim to inspire others. Except when it's silly, as in "We need a minute to call home."

OTHER WEAK SENTENCE FORMS

Intimacies: Great In the Bedroom, Poison In the Boardroom
Which of these do you say?

- ❑ I feel good about this project.

- ❑ How do you feel about it, Sam?

- ❑ Do you feel we should buy those computers?

- ❑ We feel it's wasteful.

- ❑ We studied the data and feel it supports the position.

- ❑ I feel good about your job performance.

- ❑ I'm just going to share the million dollar proposal.

- ❑ We need to get started.

- ❑ I don't like this idea.

"I" statements aren't the only gremlins that hobble leadership. In an effort to get away from old-fashioned, stiff business language, executives try to speak more informally (a great idea!). And more personally (a great idea!). They try to do so by resorting to touchy-feely words like "feel," "share," and "need" (a terrible idea!). Yes, people's sensitivities matter and workplaces should be humane and civil, but the way to make them so is not to encourage fuzzy, emotional language and the fuzzy thinking that goes with it.

Hedging Your Way to Obscurity

To hedge is literally "to hide behind words, refuse to commit oneself." Some people hedge because they don't know what they're talking about. Some hedge because they don't want others to know what they're talking about. Some hedge because they (mistakenly) believe it's a way to soften their strong personalities. Most hedge because they don't realize the degree to which hedges sap authority. Look at the list of common hedges below. Check those you use; next to each tell what impels you to speak like that.

HEDGE	REASON
❑ *Basically*	
❑ *The way I see it*	
❑ *I know that*	
❑ *Clearly*	
❑ *I guess*	
❑ *Sort of*	
❑ *I would like to know*	

Another kind of hedge exists, the one in which you not only hide behind words but diminish yourself at the same time. These hedges hurt more than the others. Check those you use and add the reasons.

HEDGE	REASON
❑ *I'm not sure how strongly I feel about it but . . .*	
❑ *I guess my question is . . .*	
❑ *I don't know anything about financial reports . . .*	
❑ *It's only my opinion but . . .*	
❑ *Because I don't know much about it . . .*	
❑ *This may be only how I feel but . . .*	
❑ *Quite honestly . . .*	
❑ *You know what I mean?*	

Then there are hedge questions:

❑ *I was just wondering . . .*	
❑ *Do you think you could . . .*	
❑ *I just wanted to know . . .*	
❑ *This is probably a stupid question . . .*	

So avoid hedges unless real uncertainty prevails; then use the strong hedges English offers: *might, may, can, should, promises, seems to, appears to.* That enables you to transform the puny "I'm not sure how I feel about it but . . ." into the authoritative but legitimately uncertain, "This prospectus seems to offer the best approach," or the legitimate question, "How did it happen?"

PUNY PASSIVES: A WORLD WITHOUT ACTORS

First, let's define the infamous passive voice. The prevailing, and sensible, way we cast English sentences uses the active voice verb: subject-verb-object (recipient of the action). Example: "The CEO wrote the talk." The voice is active because the subject or agent (The CEO) acts out the verb (wrote) and the object receives the action (the talk). Some think that active voice involves only people; that misconception encourages the passive voice. The subject (or agent) may be a person (or people) or a thing (or things). For example, "The speech brought the point home." We live in a world not only of people but of things that act: companies, products, equipment, computers (some of these act malevolently), statistics, and so on.

Here's how a passive voice verb appears. We move the object (the talk) into position at the front of the sentence or phrase, insert a "to be" verb, and move the verb over. Thus, the active voice sentence, "The CEO wrote a talk," changes into "The talk was written." Even if we add "by the CEO," the verb remains passive. Note that the passive voice always requires a version of the "to be" verb (is, are, was, were) and that not every verb can switch from the active to the passive voice. Only transitive verbs, those that can be followed by an object, can speak the active and passive voice. You don't have to know the fine points of grammar to exploit this distinction and clarify your ideas. The examples below show the difference between active and passive voice.

ACTIVE VOICE	PASSIVE VOICE
Company A won a big increase in market share.	*A big increase in market share was won by Company A.*
Please write a proposal (in this sentence, "you" is understood to be the subject).	*A proposal should be written.*
The sales manager brings new business.	*New business is brought in.*
The findings suggest an increase in pollution.	*An increase in pollution is suggested by the findings.*

In each example, the new sentence proves awkward, long, and hard to understand. However, sometimes leaders want to obfuscate or obscure meaning—then the Janus paradox prevails. For obfuscation, the passive voice may prevail: The White House often generates the famous passive, "Mistakes were made." Other occasions arise where the passive voice might work, such as when the actors are unknown (Damage was done during the break-in) or you save the agent for a strong sentence ending (The success was achieved by none other than Donald). But as a rule, prefer the active voice and the vigor of the action verb.

Two Ways to Transform Passive Voice Verbs

If your grammar checker screams "passive voice" about nearly all your sentences, your language probably doesn't inspire any followers (they probably don't even know what you're talking about or fall asleep when you speak), so consider the two ways to transform your statements. The first simply recreates the original sentence: Move the object from the subject position to its position after the verb. Here are two examples:

Passive: *The product was designed.*
Active: *Engineers designed the product.*
Passive: *The product was marketed in the south.*
Active: *We marketed the product in the south.*

The second way to transform passive sentences retains the object in the subject position and decides what it does. Here are examples.

Passive: *The product was designed.*
Active: *The product emerged from engineers' designs.*
Passive: *The product was marketed in the south.*
Active: *The product reached the southern market.*

Verbs and the Will to Act

You've seen how the passive voice drains authority; now see the central role of the action verb as a tool of leadership. Let's start with a look at the great general Ulysses S Grant,[22] at first glance an unlikely role model for executives. The historian James McPherson, in a tribute to the great Civil War general, lauds Grant's clarity of language. McPherson also asserts that Grant's battlefield success linked directly not only to his language in general but to his *action verbs* in particular. McPherson cites, "the will to act, symbolized by the prominence of active verbs in Grant's writing. . . ." For example, he quotes the order, "Pass all trains and move forward . . ." and says that such clarity "illustrates another aspect of generalship—what Grant himself called 'moral courage.' "

When you occupy the executive suite, you must give direction. The list below shows how weak communicators might have delivered Grant's direction. Check the way you'd have said it.

- ❑ *Do you think you'll get a chance to pass all trains and move forward?*

- ❑ *I expect you to pass all trains and move forward.*

- ❑ *I'm not really sure how I feel about this but I guess you should pass all trains and move forward.*

- ❑ *Um, uh, I'd like you to pass all trains and move forward.*

- ❑ *If you get a few minutes free, do you think you could pass all trains and move forward?*

- ❑ *I really need a favor from you—could you pass all trains and move forward?*

- ❑ *You people should pass all trains and move forward.*

- ❑ *Like, it'd be cool if you pass all trains and move forward.*

- ❑ *I really believe you should pass all trains and move forward.*

- ❑ *Trains should be passed and forward movement should be taken.*

- ❑ *We shall pass all trains and move forward.*

---

[22]McPherson, James, "The Unheroic Hero." *The New York Review of Books,* February 4, 1999.

❑ *Please pass all trains and move forward.* (If you're off the battlefield, the *please* improves the direction.)

Thus, action verbs don't just enliven your language—they symbolize both *moral courage* and the *will to act*, the two key elements of the language of leadership. Let's consider verbs. They do vital language jobs for us. They show action, tell of state of being, and help mark the passage of time. For our purposes, even verbs such as *know* and *understand* count as action verbs despite the fact that you don't actually act when you know or understand something. State-of-being verbs act as equal signs: they tell what things and people *are* rather than what they *do*. For example, when you say "I am the leader of the team," you use *am* as a state-of-being verb, describing what you are. If, however, you say, "I lead the team," the verb lead tells what you *do*. That's why it sounds odd to read in a resume that someone "is responsible" for the factory. That fails to tell what he does—does he run the factory, manage it, oversee its finances? If you tend to say, "The e-business program is successful," try recasting the sentence to say "The e-business program brings new prospects."

The "to be" or state-of-being verbs convey what things and people *are*. The word *am* in "I am a man" can't be replaced by any action verb—it just tells the state-of-being, which we often must do. Thus, we need state-of-being verbs, but our language falters when we use "to be" verbs when action verbs would tell the story more precisely and vividly. We say, "It is very important," when we should have said, *It matters* or *It counts*.

As the proportion of action versus "to be" verbs grows, select the most precise verb to clarify the story. Move from the vague *impact* to the precise *hurt* or *helped* or *damaged* or *grew*. Note that the precise verb isn't the longest (although it might be). Winston Churchill said, "The short words are best." This book, then, asserts that action verbs endow leaders' communications with moral courage, clarity, and brevity. Lead in the executive suite because you have the will and the power to act, as your action verbs reveal.

Language That Persuades

Why bother shedding weak language and acquiring strong forms and action verbs if not to persuade? If you wish to have followers, you must persuade them to do what is right. If you wish to sell anything, you must persuade customers to buy it. All the work you've done so far helps you persuade. Now learn skills that enable you to control various persuasive techniques.

If you belong to the sledgehammer school of persuasion, you're in the wrong place. But if you aim for civil persuasion, consider columnist Ellen Goodman's recommendation:

> You have to make your point by leading others through the merits of your case, and showing how you reached your conclusions. You won't win skeptics over by force-feeding them your point of view. You have to bring other people through the argument, so it's not you saying, "This is what I think, asshole." You have to bring them through the argument to show respect for the opposition. You also have to show how your mind is working so they will run with you, even if they don't come to the same conclusion. . . . Shrillness doesn't work. You have to ask what you want. What is your goal? Do you want to make your point, do you want people to listen to you, or do you want to vent? If you want to vent, go home, get into the shower and scream. If you want to have a public argument in which people will actually listen to you, get a grip.[23]

How, exactly, can you get a grip on persuasive techniques? Research helps. Social psychologists have experimented with various persuasive techniques that can help you influence others. Robert Cialdini,[24] Regents' Professor of Psychology at Arizona State University, recommends six tendencies of human behavior that come into play in generating a positive response. He performed experiments that compared persuasiveness with and without appealing to these

---

[23]Germer, Fawn, *Hard Won Wisdom.* New York: Perigee, 2001.

[24]Cialdini, Robert, "The Science of Persuasion." *Scientific American,* February 2001, pp. 76–81. www.influenceatwork.com

tendencies. For example, people tend to be persuaded by those they like. An excellent example came up when President Ronald Reagan died. Even his opponents who disagreed with him on every political issue liked him and tried to work with him. After reading about them in this section, explore how you can use these techniques as a leader, on the podium, and in writing.

SIX WAYS TO GENERATE POSITIVE RESPONSES

Reciprocation

The "code of reciprocity" obligates individuals to repay in kind what they have received. That's why charitable organizations and businesses give away so many free samples. But reciprocity includes more than gifts and favors; it also applies to concessions that people make to one another. That's the principle behind negotiation: "I yield a concession to you and you do so for me." Can you see a way to include reciprocity in the executive suite, in your language?

_____

_____

_____

Consistency

If you can get people to make a public commitment to your cause, it's easier to persuade them to fulfill that commitment. In one experiment, a restaurant sought to reduce its reservation no-show rate. Their ordinary request, "Please call if you have to change your plans," didn't get people to cancel and resulted in empty tables. Simply changing the wording to say, "Will you please call if you have to change your plans?" and waiting for a reply reduced the no-show rate by two thirds. Can you think of ways you can ask people to make public commitments to what must be done? Can you add language like that to meetings and presentations?

_____

_____

_____

Social Validation

Letting people know that others do something encourages them to do the same. Experiments show that a group of people standing in the street looking at the sky results in others stopping to do the same. Can you think of ways you can do that to increase your persuasive power?

_____

_____

_____

Liking

The simple positive connection between people implied in the word *liking* proves a powerful persuasive force: people are more likely to go along with someone they like. Cialdini gives as example the worldwide popularity of Tupperware parties, in which people buy from a friend rather than a stranger. Physical attractiveness, similarity, compliments, and cooperation encourage the liking that affects behavior. Think of the times you walked through a shop and the salesperson commented favorably on a piece of your clothing—you're more likely to buy from that salesperson. In one experiment, solicitors on a college campus found that charity donations doubled when they added the phrase "I'm a student, too" to their request. Can you think of ways you can persuade your audiences through liking, physical attractiveness, similarity, compliments, and cooperation?

_____

_____

_____

Authority

In one experiment, a man tripled the number of people who would follow him across the street against the light by "changing one simple thing. Instead of casual dress, he donned markers of authority; a suit and tie." Remember that when you consider your own trappings in the executive suite. Of course, your experience and background, woven into a presentation, also endows you with authority (remember: no bragging!!) Can you think of other ways you can increase your authority?

_____

_____

_____

Scarcity

Perceived scarcity affects judgment: items and opportunities become more desirable to us as they become less available. If you've ever broken a piece of your old china and sought to replace it after it's out of production, you've learned that painful lesson. And "scarcity affects the value not only of commodities but of information as well. Information that is exclusive is more persuasive." Can you exploit this information to add to your persuasiveness in the executive suite?

_____

_____

_____

Professor Cialdini's insights will appear again when we discuss meetings, speech writing, and negotiating.

With these ideas as a backdrop, let's examine the language techniques that enable you to persuade and influence others.

RHETORIC—EIGHT USEFUL TOOLS

Your language gains power each time you shed a weak word or sentence form and replace it with a strong word or sentence form,. But leadership demands rhetorical tools that persuade, inspire, and teach others. Although *rhetoric* has gotten a bad name ("It's only rhetoric"), its definition, "skill in using language effectively and persuasively," reflects the reason you bought this book. Kathleen Hall Jamieson notes, "Rhetoric makes sense of otherwise inchoate experiences. It structures. It orders. It focuses." Analysis of any good speech or presentation shows that its writer understood and applied the various rhetorical techniques. We'll cover eight techniques here and give examples and models—master these and add others as you gain increasing control over the language of leadership. Names appearing in parentheses are the authors.

Parallelism

The American Heritage Dictionary defines *parallelism* as "the use of identical or equivalent syntactic constructions in corresponding clauses." That technical definition simply means that parallels enable you to show relationships among ideas through relationships among the words in sentences and on lists. Parallels can comprise a simple series in a list of items, an enumerated series in an entire piece, or a string of sentences linked by similar forms. And each parallel can open with any part of speech. In *The Practical Stylist,*[25] Sheridan Baker writes, "Use parallels wherever you can. This is what parallel thinking brings—balance and control and an eye for sentences that seem intellectual totalities." These intellectual totalities imbue every statement, every slide, every list with clarity and power. They also add efficiency: parallels yield greater meaning per word than other language forms. But parallels don't come easy: you must understand the concept, select coordinate ideas, and construct the parallels. The ear proves a useful guide: read the sentence or list aloud to hear whether you attained parallels. When you start out, you may prefer to copy the models below. The political models come from speeches by Abraham Lincoln, Tony Blair, and Martin Luther King, Jr.

- *How We Gained Market Share*

   Television ads
   Web links
   Newspaper stories
   Lead generation

- *John excels at reading, writing, speaking, and listening.*

- *. . . that government of the people, by the people, for the people shall not perish . . .* (Lincoln)

- *We were all reared on battles between great warriors, between great nations, between powerful forces and ideologies . . .* (Blair)

---

[25]Baker, Sheridan, *The Practical Stylist, 2nd ed.* New York: Crowell, 1969.

- *With this faith we will be able to work together, to pray together, to struggle together, to stand up for freedom together . . .* (King)

- *So let freedom ring from the prodigious hilltops of New Hampshire. Let freedom ring from the mighty mountains of New York. Let freedom ring from the heightening Alleghenies of Pennsylvania.* (King)

Balance

Balance is a form of parallelism—balanced sentences match beginning and ending phrases:

- *Washington is a city of northern charm and southern efficiency.* (John F. Kennedy)

- *Our ultimate weapon is not our guns, but our beliefs.* (Blair)

- *Finishing the fighting is not finishing the job.* (Blair)

- *When we removed the Taliban and Saddam Hussein, this was not imperialism. For these oppressed people, it was their liberation.* (Blair)

Enumeration

Enumeration is the easiest rhetorical tool in your kit. You can organize a single sentence, a paragraph, or an entire piece with this simple device, which also works as an economical transition. The only caveat: don't use the same enumeration twice within a piece.

- *Here's how to proceed: first, empty the building; second, call the fire department; third, inform the police.*

- *This talk discusses three key points. First, we examine the decline in profit. Second, we report the reasons. Third, we suggest the solutions.*

Rhetorical Question

Another excellent organizing device, the rhetorical question is one to which you don't expect an answer from the audience. Rhetorical questions work so well because they're always in parallel.

- *We face two crucial questions. How did we get to this impasse? How can we change our procedures?*

- *Today's talk answers three questions. Why do we require the new initiative? What is the new initiative? How shall we implement it in this department?*

Tricolon

Tricolon is simply the rule of three: eyes and ears like threes. If the information can be grouped in threes, group it that way. Indeed, most of the models above use tricolon. Threes show that you care about the audience's understanding and took the trouble to group your ideas.

- *. . . we mutually pledge our lives, our fortunes, and our sacred honor.* (Declaration of Independence)

- *. . . will serve our customers, our salespeople, and our distributors.*

Simile

Similes suggest that one thing is like another. Similes bring clarity to abstract or difficult information.

- *Our meetings are like circuses.*

- *My management team is like a kindergarten.*

- *A vision statement is like a blueprint.*

- *This momentous decree came as a great beacon light of hope . . .* (King)

Metaphor

Metaphor speaks as though one thing were another. Metaphors clarify abstract ideas and make them concrete. Extended metaphors pursue the same likeness throughout the piece.

- *In a sense, we have come to our nation's capital to cash a check.* (King)

- *When the architects of the republic wrote the magnificent words of the Constitution and the Declaration of Independence, they were signing a promissary note to which every American was to fall heir.* (King)

- *A new and deadly virus has emerged. The virus is terrorism . . .* (Blair)

- *(America should never be a land of)* "*small dreams*" (Reagan)

- *Human freedom is on the march.* (Reagan)

Alliteration

The dictionary defines alliteration as "The repetition of the same consonant sounds . . . at the beginning of words. . . ." For example, the famous *nattering nabobs of negativism*. We don't get many opportunities to alliterate but know about it should the occasion arise. William Safire[26] gives wonderful examples: "past the partisan politics of the past," "enlightened engagement," "principled partnerships," "muscular multilateralism," "war on work," "driven us back into the days of deficits, debt, and doubt," "slavishly spewed sound bites," "crime, corruption, and cronies; bossism, blundering, and bungling," and, finally, "not heroics but healing; not nostrums but normalcy; not revolution but restoration; not agitation but adjustment; not surgery but serenity. . . ." Our leadership students have come up with some fine examples, proving that you don't require a speech writer to speak well: "people, positions, parameters," and "complicated, complex, and convoluted." Carry alliteration in your quiver of rhetorical tools; use it when the opportunity arises.

SENTENCES THAT:

Lead

All the rhetorical devices can apply to every spoken and written communication. You now have the tools to create sentences that accomplish the purposes of leadership. You'll find models below. Copy the forms, changing the words so they fit your situation. Model sentences appear later in this book as well.

---

[26]Safire, William, "Aggie Award," the *New York Times,* October 12, 2003.

Inspire

You bring great talent to this job. You bring great enthusiasm. You bring all the elements to ensure our success.

_____

_____

_____

Let the word go forth from this time and place—to friend and foe alike—that the torch has been passed to a new generation of Americans, born in this century, tempered by war, disciplined by a hard and bitter peace, proud of our ancient heritage and unwilling to witness or permit the slow undoing of those human rights to which this nation has always been committed, and to which we are committed today, at home and around the world. (John F. Kennedy)

Nurture

This talent promises to enrich the engineering team. Warm good wishes to you.

_____

_____

_____

Say No

The rules prevent us from fulfilling that request, refunding the fee, or changing the procedure.

That's not possible (doable, legal, efficient).

The budget won't allow for a raise this year.

_____

_____

_____

Criticize

That kind of behavior damages morale, prevents people from working together, and leads to dismissal.

_____

_____

_____

Show Anger

We shall not accept an economy that strips the poor of their dignity, that enriches the wealthy at the expense of the poor, that deprives the elderly of health care.

That xxx is not acceptable (tolerable, permissible, legal).

WORDS: PUNY AND POWERFUL

Mark Twain notes, "The right word is to the almost right word as lightning is to the lightning bug." The difference between an ordinary utterance and one that leads lies in choosing lightning words, not lightning bugs. Action verbs comprise a whole class of lightning words—simply replacing "to be" verbs with action verbs sparks your language. And many examples of lightning bugs drag down language in the executive suite. Note on the list below that the switch from the weak to the powerful replaces the vague with the precise, the long with the short.

LIGHTNING BUGS— Long and Vague	LIGHTNING WORDS— Short and Smart
Facilitate	Ease, speed
Tangibilize	Make
Reprioritize	Set priorities
Endpoint environmental direction	Aim, goal

Long and Vague	Short and Smart
Proactive	Foresighted
Customize	Fit, tailor
Impact	Affect, influence, shape
Share	Explain, describe, detail, report
Conceptualization	Idea
Develop	Design, create, generate
Very, very important	Critical, essential, vital, central
As soon as possible	By September 16th
Just (as in I'm just going to share . . .)	Omit it
Need (except when applied to food, warmth, or love)	Require, demand, must

Jargon

You can't have a conversation about words in the executive suite without talking about jargon. Just what is jargon and how does it help or hinder you? The second edition of *The Random House Dictionary* defines *jargon* in two ways: it's "vocabulary peculiar to a particular trade, profession, or group," and it's also "unintelligible or meaningless talk or writing." What determines whether any particular term is helpful or hurtful jargon? The audience! As you tell your company's story to various audiences, decide which audiences will understand vocabulary peculiar to the trade or profession and which audiences will simply find it unintelligible. An insurance executive learned his expensive lesson about jargon when he used an in-house term to describe partial liability coverage to a client; the client misunderstood and thought he had full coverage. When he learned the truth, he cancelled the whole contract. Jargon can kill.

Do It Now!

Ask the three questions about each of the sentences. Recast them, replacing the emotional words with powerful nouns and verbs.

I feel good about this project.

What is it not about?

_____

What is it about? (Subject)

_____

What does it do? (Prefer action verb)

_____

How do you feel about it, Sam?

What is it not about?

_____

What is it about? (Subject)

_____

What does it do? (Prefer action verb)

_____

Do you feel we should buy those computers?

What is it not about?

_____

What is it about? (Subject)

_____

What does it do? (Prefer action verb)

_____

We feel it's wasteful.

What is it not about?

_____

What is it about? (Subject)

_____

What does it do? (Prefer action verb)

_____

We studied the data and feel it supports the position.

What is it not about?

_____

What is it about? (Subject)

_____

What does it do? (Prefer action verb)

_____

I feel good about your job performance.

What is it not about?

_____

What is it about? (Subject)

_____

What does it do? (Prefer action verb)

_____

I'm just going to share the million dollar proposal.

What is it not about?

_____

What is it about? (Subject)

_____

What does it do? (Prefer action verb)

_____

We need to get started.

What is it not about?

_____

What is it about? (Subject)

_____

What does it do? (Prefer action verb)

_____

I don't like this idea.

What is it not about?

_____

What is it about? (Subject)

_____

What does it do? (Prefer action verb)

_____

Do It Now!

Ask the three questions to transform *I like that idea* from a personal, self-centered, vague sentence into one that endows you with authority.

What is it not about? _____

What is it about? _____

What does it do? _____

Do It Now!

Review your transcript and a written piece. Circle the lightning bugs and replace them with lightning words.

Get a good dictionary and check precise definitions of words you overuse.

Look for jargon in your e-mails. Decide if each example is positive or negative jargon.

You're well on your way to the language of leadership. Ideas, reading, listening, body language, persuasion, rhetoric, sentences, and words advance your quest. Yet communication demands clear and compelling complete pieces as well: talks, presentations, speeches, e-mails, letters, proposals, and reports. The next chapters discuss structures, stressing those that advance your leadership role. Finally, we'll cruise step by step through a no fail way to organize every written and spoken presentation.

7

BUILDING STURDY STRUCTURES

*The first principle of composition . . . is to foresee or determine the
shape of what is to come and pursue that shape.* —E. B. WHITE

Why does e-mail steal your time? Why do presentations bore you? Why don't
your proposals win? Why do your talks fall flat? Because they lack structure.
Their creators meant to get ideas across but failed. Indeed the creators may
have sunk endless hours of preparation into their duds. But building a communication without structure builds a house of straw.

An Introduction to Structures

If communications are buildings that stand strong and straight, think of yourself as the architect. Just as buildings have *required*, *optional*, and *decorative*
structures, so communications have required, optional, and decorative structures. For example, foundations and roofs are required, windows and elevators
are optional, and paint and wallpaper are decorative. Certain structures are required in some communications, optional in others. For example, the heading
(or title) is required in e-mail but optional in letters.

The Lead

The lead opens the piece, optional in e-mail but required in spoken presentations and most formal writing. Not actually part of the piece, the lead serves two purposes: to engage the audience and to establish your credibility as one worth listening to (or reading). It offers the opportunity to break through the barriers that separate you from the audience. They include physical barriers of distance, equipment, or room layout; psychological barriers of unfamiliarity, bias against your appearance or something you represent; or differences in educational or professional level. The lead can also begin to introduce the content, especially in a business presentation. And, because the lead stands separate from the rest of the piece, you can reuse letters and speeches by varying their leads to fit different audiences.

An executive faced a singular issue for an upcoming presentation. She had accepted a senior marketing position in a high-tech manufacturing firm in Atlanta, Georgia. She was the first woman ever in this job and the first African-American, and this was her first introduction to those who would report to her. This lead mattered more than most. The first few sentences of her talk never used an "I" statement but rather told of her pride at the opportunity to work with such an accomplished team She named several audience members and mentioned their contributions, thereby establishing her own authority. Then people listened as she spoke of her plans.

EIGHT WAYS TO LEAD A TALK

Set the pace in the lead; it quickly tells the audience whether you'll interest and enliven, whether you have authority, whether they'll gain anything from giving you their valuable time and attention. My study of leads reveals that they often refer to the audience, time, place, or language. They also may predict the content of the speech. Both persuasive and rhetorical tools may show up in the lead (or anywhere else in the piece for that matter). Here are varied leads you can emulate by changing a few words:

1. Thank the host organization:

Thanks to the organizing committee, the American Association of Medical Colleges, and especially to Jan Jones for her gracious introduction.

2. Refer generously to the host, city or audience:

Mr. Vice President, Mr. Speaker, members of the Senate and the House of Representatives of the United States: In fulfilling my duty to report on the state of the Union, I am proud to say to you that the spirit of the American people was never higher than it is today. The Union was never more closely knit together and the country was never more deeply determined to face the solemn tasks before it. (Franklin D. Roosevelt)

An invitation to come to Orlando from Rochester during January always gets a warm welcome—what a delight it is to bask in the warm sun of your beautiful city.

An engineering director always seeks to work with exceptional people, and you represent the best of the field. Charlie Jones designed the first xxx in the world; Bill Mathews led the fastest quality control team in the west; Darnelle Williams created what has become the prototype for all widgets.

What a delight to speak to professional and business people who donate time and money to Mercy Flights. Your generosity has enabled 235 people to receive the lifesaving medical care they required.

As we begin our address to this audience, which is unique in the world, we wish to express our profound gratitude to U Thant, your Secretary General, for the invitation which he extended to us to visit the United Nations, on the occasion of the twentieth anniversary of the foundation of this world institution for peace and for collaboration between the peoples of the entire earth. (Pope Paul VI)

3. Give an overview of the speech:

*Tonight I want to talk to you about my hope for the future, my faith in the American people, and my vision of the kind of country we can build together. (*William Jefferson Clinton, Acceptance Speech*)*

4. Refer to time or language (or both):

*I do not propose to say many words tonight. The time has come when action rather than speech is required. (*Neville Chamberlain*)*

5. Tell an apt anecdote:

Everyone loves a good story. A lead story must be short, interesting, and clearly linked to the business purpose of the speech.

Efforts to open world markets hit quite choppy waters in 1993. Both NAFTA and the Uruguay round negotiations were stridently attacked by those who wanted to hang on to their protections and could not be persuaded of the perils of their course.

Indeed they reminded me of the vice-admiral that was commanding a battleship in the North Atlantic on a particularly stormy night who saw a light coming toward his vessel and sent a radio message, "Give way and move twenty degrees south" and immediately a message came back, "Give way and you move twenty degrees north." The vice-admiral was not used to having his orders disobeyed, so he thought there might be some confusion. He sent the same message again and immediately, the message came back. "You give way and move twenty degrees north." This time he was very perturbed and he sent a very precise message: "I am a vice-admiral commanding a battleship and I order you to give way and move twenty degrees south." And this time there was a long pause, but the message came back, "I am a seaman first class. I am manning a lighthouse." (pause for laughter)

*And so while we can breathe a sigh of relief that we avoided the rocks and shoals in the 1993, many of the underlying issues that challenged us in the last year are still with us. (*Carla Hills, Commonwealth Club of California*)*

6. Open with an interesting quotation:

Add a few books of quotations to your business library and Web preferences, and check them for apt words about the topic you're going to discuss. Next, start a computer file of quotations that you can use in future talks. Quotations add punch to the talk. They tap the common core of shared experience. They suggest that you tune in to the same people and ideas your audience tunes in to. If addressing an audience in another country, quote from that country's history or literature: it's a gracious way of saying you care about this audience. One speaker was delivering a talk about conversations. He led with this quotation: "I've heard the expression 'he talks too much' but did you ever hear, 'he listens too much?' " What a great way to talk about listening!

You'll find below a list of quotations that can lead almost any speech. Add to this list and keep your quotations handy.

We must think anew and act anew. We must disenthrall ourselves. (Abraham Lincoln)

If you have an important point to make, don't try to be subtle or clever. Use a pile driver. (Winston Churchill)

Leadership, like life, can only be learned as you go along. (Harold Geneen)

The person who knows "how" will always have a job. The person who knows "why" will always be his boss. (Diane Ravitch)

I start with the premise that the function of leadership is to produce more leaders, not more followers. (Ralph Nader)

When there is no vision, the people perish. (Bible, Proverbs 29: 19)

Strategic planning is worthless—unless there is first a strategic vision. (John Naisbitt)

The opposite of talking isn't listening. The opposite of talking is waiting. (Fran Lebowitz)

Never tell a story because it is true: tell it because it is a good story. (John Mahaffy)

Money is like promises—easier made than kept. (Josh Billings)

You don't need an MBA from Harvard to figure out how to lose money. (Royal Little)

I have enough money to last me the rest of my life, unless I buy something. (Jackie Mason)

The by-product is sometimes more valuable than the product. (Havelock Ellis)

When the best leader's work is done, the people say, "We did it ourselves." (Lao-Tzu)

Work smarter, not harder. (Anonymous)

Definition of a manager: a man who never puts off till tomorrow that which he can get someone else to do today. (Anonymous)

Watch the turtle. He only moves forward by sticking his neck out. (Louis V. Gerstner, Jr.)

Always do what you are afraid to do. (Ralph Waldo Emerson)

7. Refer or allude to a commonly known book or experience:

Two great speakers from American history model the value of quotation and allusion. An allusion is an indirect reference in which you don't specifically identify the source. An allusion can use a few of the same words as in the original or it can paraphrase a commonly known reference.

Abraham Lincoln opened the *Gettysburg Address,* *"Four score and seven years ago. . . ."* He wasn't quoting directly from the Bible, but he was alluding to it; he knew that everyone in the audience read the Bible and would be familiar with those words. Those six words, then, tapped a common core of shared allusion, and bridged the chasm between speaker and audience. A hundred years later, Martin Luther King, Jr. opened the "I Have a Dream" speech by alluding to Lincoln: *"Five score years ago. . . ."* With only four words, King placed himself squarely in the American and the biblical traditions.

8. Define or discuss a relevant word:

Almost any reference to language can lead a talk. Try looking up a key word in an unabridged dictionary. Learn the different parts of speech, the word's usage history, the components of the word. These informative tidbits spice the talk. One executive works in the "wet copying" division of Xerox and was invited to keynote a meeting of the "wet copying" association. In her search for an interesting lead, she asked help from someone who knows how to find out about the history of Greek word parts. She learned that, although the prefix xer- means "dry," in its early history it also referred to a container to hold wet liquids. What an interesting lead for her speech!

A language consultant was asked to deliver a workshop at a convention for allergists. Seeking to engage the doctors and add a touch of humor, the consultant first read handouts and literature for allergists. Allergists read a lot about dust, which is composed of some very unpleasant things: fly wings, bodies of little dead creatures, and so on. The consultant simply led the talk by saying he looked for professional words in the dictionary, so he sought the meaning of "dust." The allergists laughed and warmed immediately to the presentation. Of course, no other group would find the word "dust" funny.

A marketing expert decided to check out the commonly used word "branding." The discovery that the first use of branding applied to cattle produced a funny and engaging lead to the talk.

Do It Now!

Start a word-processing file of quotations that you might use in future presentations. Find Web sites with useful quotations in your field.

Check the ways you might lead upcoming talks. On the lines below indicate what you might say. Be sure to use the sentence forms, persuasive techniques, and rhetorical devices covered so far.

Thank the host organization.

_____

_____

_____

Refer generously to the host, city or audience.

_____

_____

_____

Give an overview of the speech.

_____

_____

_____

Refer to time or language (or both).

_____

_____

_____

Tell an apt anecdote.

_____

_____

_____

Open with an interesting quotation.

_____

_____

_____

Refer or allude to a commonly known book or experience.

_____

_____

_____

Define or discuss a relevant word.

_____

_____

_____

TWO WAYS *NOT* TO LEAD A TALK

Whatever else you say, do not demean yourself; do not apologize; do not say "This will be long and boring" or "I'm so sorry—I didn't have enough time to prepare" or "You probably can't see these slides." Don't suggest that it's not worthwhile to listen to you.

And be leery of jokes. Unless you're naturally funny or are absolutely confident that your joke won't insult anyone, avoid this lead.

All the leads can also open written communications; however, a lead is not always required in writing. For example, most e-mails do not require leads.

The Thesis Statement: Keystone Structure

Let's define the *thesis statement:* "the proposition that the writer details, defends, or explains in the piece." It *must* comprise one or more complete sentences, not a phrase or title. Think of the thesis statement as an umbrella covering both the purpose and the topics of the talk or piece of writing, in their proper sequence. The thesis clearly conveys the big picture, not the details. Of all the sentences in your piece, the thesis statement should get your best effort; make it well-reasoned and well-written. Use whatever you've learned about persuasion and rhetoric to write this keystone structure that may prove to be the only thing the audience remembers! Failed communications do so in part because they lack clear thesis statements or because the thesis is in the wrong place.

Do It Now!

Here are sample thesis statements. You can copy the forms and insert the words that fit your talk. On the lines below each, recast the sentence(s) as if they could appear in one of your own messages.

For the next twenty minutes, we'll discuss (review, analyze, detail, look at, view) the project status to date, detail the problems, and suggest improvements in the process.

_____

_____

_____

Today's talk examines the benefits of the xxx, describes the disadvantages, and urges you to adopt xxx.

The engineering department continues to develop new design procedures to save 10 percent in the manufacturing process. This talk gives you the status, explains the challenges we face, and suggests three possible solutions.

Hermetic Science's experience, expertise, and availability make us the ideal consultants for your project. We'll review our background and show how it dovetails with your ambitions, how your firm benefits from it, and how your productivity will rise by at least 20 percent.

What is the language of leadership? This talk defines it, shows seven specific applications in the global marketplace, and seeks your approval of the leadership initiative.

For the next twenty minutes, we'll answer these questions: First, what is the background of the web design initiative? Second, how can our management group support it? Finally, how will it affect our bottom line? Then we have a ten-minute question period and two minutes to sum up.

_____

_____

_____

Please note that convention permits speakers to hold the thesis till the end of the talk. Lyndon Johnson did. In 1968, he addressed the nation about the Vietnam War. Here's his shocking end paragraph.

I shall not seek, and I will not accept, the nomination of my party for another term as your President. But let men everywhere know, however, that a strong and a confident and a vigilant America stands ready tonight to seek an honorable peace; and stands ready tonight to defend an honored cause, whatever the price, whatever the burden, whatever the sacrifice that duty may require. Thank you for listening. Good night and God bless you all.

Increase the chance of being understood: stick to the principle of an early and clear thesis statement. And memorable communicators don't just tell their thesis statements; they repeat or rephrase that thesis often enough to be remembered.

The Internal Structures: Topic Sentences, Transitions, and Reminders

The internal structures reveal the logic of the piece and link one section to the next. You know the big ideas of your topics. You know how they link to each another, but your audience doesn't. Topic sentences introduce the big ideas of your presentation and show the relationships between these ideas and the thesis. Strong topic sentences endow your talk with fluency, which is missing in almost all business and professional communications. In writing, the reader knows when a new paragraph begins: he sees an indentation, a roman numeral, an underlined heading, and a topic sentence. In speaking, of course, the listener lacks those signals; you as the speaker indicate the beginnings of new topics. Do so through sentence form, by enumeration, via transitions, or on visuals.

Each paragraph has a topic sentence that tells its main premise and shows the logical transition from the last paragraph. The addition of a transitional word or phrase can help the topic sentence both to tell the main premise and provide the transition.

Here are words and phrases that smooth transitions:

USEFUL TRANSITION WORDS AND PHRASES

and	again	while
just as . . . so	but	nevertheless
also	yet	therefore
moreover	still	as a result
second	even so	since
third	at the same time	because
in addition	although	thus
furthermore	despite	accordingly
more specifically	however	unfortunately

Listeners' memories limit what they can follow. You can be even more helpful by using the transition as a review of what you just said, then telling the next topic. Here are examples.

New topic:
Here's how we handled the marketing problem.

New topic and transition:
Once we understood its magnitude, here's how we handled the marketing problem.

New topic, transition, and review of previous paragraph:
Having resolved the issues of packaging, we learned of our 60 percent loss of market share. Here's how we handled the marketing problem.

Structures that End

End with one or more of the structures listed here. The choice of structures depends on the length, formality, and complexity of the piece. The transition shows that the end is in sight.

SUM UP, REVIEW

The review simply reminds people of what you spoke about. It can list main ideas you covered:

> *In sum, today's session covered the seven elements of a successful financial outlook: the xxx, which . . . ; the xxx, which . . . ; the xxx, which . . . ; the xxx, which . . . ; the xxx, which . . . ; the xxx, which. . . .*

> *To sum up, we've explored the crystalline elements in the chemical reaction: the xxx, the xxx, and the xxx.*

> *All in all, we've reviewed the June financial data for all departments and suggested five improvements for next quarter: (1), (2), (3), (4), and (5).*

CALL TO ACTION

If you want your audience to do something, tell them specifically what, and when:

> *In sum, the team recommends that we adopt the Venus program from Galaxie company. Please approve the request by December 10.*

Now that you've seen all the benefits of the lunar equipment, please approve the purchase order on your desk.

Abraham Lincoln said, "We must think anew and act anew." We too must think anew, act anew, and even speak anew as we venture into the global world of commerce.

END STRONGLY

Add unity by ending as you opened, or varying the opening slightly. Bill Clinton's acceptance speech at the 1992 Democratic Convention led with a reference to hope. Here's his end:

I end tonight where it all began for me: I still believe in a place called Hope.

Here are strong endings. Some call to act.

We have to keep in mind at all times that we are not fighting for integration, nor are we fighting for segregation. We are fighting for the right to live as free humans in society. In fact, we are actually fighting for rights that are even greater than civil rights and that is human rights. (Malcolm X)

And so, my fellow Americans: ask not what your country can do for you—ask what you can do for your country.
My fellow citizens of the world, ask not what America will do for you, but what together we can do for the freedom of man.
Finally, whether you are citizens of America or citizens of the world, ask of us here the same high standards of strength and sacrifice which we ask of you. With a good conscience our only sure reward, with history the final judge of our deeds, let us go forth to lead the land we love, asking His blessing and His help, but knowing that here on earth God's work must truly be our own. (John F. Kennedy)

To all the peoples of the world, I once more give expression to America's prayerful and continuing aspiration:

We pray that people of all faiths, all races, all nations, may have their great human needs satisfied; that those now denied opportunity shall come to enjoy it to the full; that all who yearn for freedom may experience its spiritual blessings; that those who have freedom will understand, also, its heavy responsibilities; that all who are insensitive to the needs of others will learn charity; that the scourges of poverty, disease and ignorance will be made to disappear from the earth; and that in the goodness of time, all peoples will come to live together in a peace guaranteed by the binding force of mutual respect and love. . . . Thank you, and good night. (Dwight D. Eisenhower)

And when this happens and when we allow freedom to ring, and when we let it ring from every village and every hamlet, from every state and every city, we will be able to speed up that day when all God's children, black men and white men, Jews and Gentiles, Protestants and Catholics, will be able to join hands and sing in the words of that old Negro spiritual, "Free at last! Free at last! Thank God almighty, we are free at last." (Martin Luther King, Jr.)

Do It Now!

On the lines below, write an ending you might use in an upcoming presentation.

_____

_____

_____

In sum, structures pay in five ways: they cut preparation time; they save reading time; they establish credibility; they show your leadership talent; they force you to think clearly. They equip you to lead.

8

ORGANIZING SPOKEN AND WRITTEN COMMUNICATIONS

He is one of those orators of whom it was well said, "Before they get up, they do not know what they are going to say; when they are speaking, they do not know what they are saying; and when they have sat down, they do not know what they have said."

—Winston Churchill

You know the various structures, but how do you craft them for your own presentation?

Remember the old joke about how you face more problems than the president: he worries about war, peace, and the economy; you worry about war, peace, the economy, how to get to work on time, how to get the laundry done, and much more. Well, you face more problems than other speakers and writers: they worry about clarity, brevity, and persuasion. You worry about clarity, brevity, persuasion, inspiration, authority, credibility, and more. The president also has a team of speech writers and the trappings of the Oval Office. What do you have?

Well, you may have a team of speech writers or a single hired consultant. Or you may have to rely on yourself alone. Either way, get a running start by understanding how to plan and organize written and spoken communications: remember that persuasiveness shows up in all lists of leadership attributes. In the pages that follow, you'll meet a way to organize that has helped leaders persuade, inspire, and earn authority. It's certainly not the only way—if you're a skilled speaker and writer and have a technique that succeeds, stick with it. If you usually organize by looking at a blank screen, just starting to type, or, worse, just starting to talk, take a couple of hours to learn a logical way to put ideas into words and visuals.

Do It Now!

Read "The Organization System" in its entirety. Next, follow it to plan a piece you have to write or speak at work. In a future chapter you'll see The Organization System at work.

The Organization System

STEP 1 THINK ABOUT THE AUDIENCE.

Get this step right—most communication disasters happen because a speaker or writer neglected to consider the audience. The executive who opens with a dirty joke or offensive remark, the CEO who demeans staff members, and the leader who speaks jargon fail because they missed Step 1. Are your listeners men, women, Americans, expatriates, immigrants, college graduates, high school dropouts, people with particular sensibilities? Are they your age, older, or younger? Likely to agree with or oppose your position? If the piece you're planning matters, take a moment to jot down a few notes about the audience.

If the communication is an e-mail, note that the audience may grow beyond those you think you'll reach—the worst e-mails (and sometimes the best) can circulate widely.

STEP 2 DETERMINE THE PURPOSE(S).

What should this missive do? Knowing precisely what you aim to accomplish increases the chance of success and decreases the chance of rambling. Each purpose starts with an action verb.

- **Alert** audience to value of new procedures

- **Propose** marketing initiative

- **Clarify** meaning of hiring policy

- **Compare** profits of last two years

- **Demonstrate** value of staff increase

- **Enlist** support for economy measures

- **Explain** reasons for budget increases

- **Foster** international relationships

- **Inform** about new procedures

- **Initiate** mentor program

- **Inspire** greater effort

- **Introduce** new executive vice president

- **Motivate** productivity growth

- **Persuade** to adopt new system

- **Report** progress year to date on budget cuts

- **Review** survey findings

- **Suggest** new leadership program

- **Support** incentive program

STEP 3 LIST THE DETAILS.

At this point, the Organization System begins to differ from other approaches—it's a bottom-up rather than a top-down method. Rather than determining the big topics you'll cover, brain storm or brain dump every detail that might advance the purposes. Lay them out (on little sticky notes or on the screen in a program like PowerPoint) so you can see them all. The logical process here involves *analysis*, or breaking down big ideas into their small components.

STEP 4 GROUP THE DETAILS.

Robert Louis Stevenson said, "A man who can group his ideas is a good writer." The logical process here is *synthesis*—we discussed synthesis as the highest level reading skill. Here it engages a high level of creative reasoning, a crucial aspect of leadership ability. Move the details around, considering which combinations advance the purposes. You can group the details in many ways, some unexpected; for example, financial data and employment figures may advance your purposes better if presented together. And you may want to remove some details that fell out of your brain in Step 3.

STEP 5 ORDER THE DETAILS.

Within the groups, decide the order of details.

STEP 6 NAME THE TOPICS.

Now you have ordered groups of details; these now comprise the big ideas, or topics, of your communication (if you're writing a book, they'll grow into chapters). Give each topic a title, as though they are chapters in a book. For example, topics might include Where We Came From, How We Started, Where We're Going.

STEP 7 ORDER THE TOPICS.

Decide the best order in which to present the topics. For example, the three topics above can be presented in any sequence; it's a fine idea to discuss Where We're Going before discussing How We Started. This frees you from dullness.

STEP 8 WRITE THE THESIS STATEMENT.

Now that you know the purposes, topics, and order, write the thesis statement. Use powerful sentence forms and rhetoric (use the models in the last chapter).

Sometimes the purposes combine to make a tricolon in parallel, as in "Today we review the first quarter results, discuss plans for the second quarter, and enlist your support in our efforts to gain market share next year."

STEP 9 WRITE THE LEAD AND END STRUCTURES.

Recall that the lead isn't really part of the piece—it can vary with various audiences. In writing, the lead is optional; in speaking the lead is required. If you prepare the end structures as well, you should find it easier to complete the internal structures.

STEP 10 PLAN THE PARAGRAPHS, TOPIC SENTENCES, TRANSITIONS, AND REMINDERS.

The piece now has its skeleton in place. All that remains is to put the flesh on the bones.

STEP 11 COMPLETE THE PIECE.

Write every word, whether the final product is spoken or written.

STEP 12 SPEAKING: CREATE THE VISUAL AIDS.

Writing: Edit and rewrite.

Till now, the system is the same for speaking and writing.

STEP 13 SPEAKING: REHEARSE.

Writing: Proofread.

Later you'll walk through the Organization System in detail for an actual talk. You've met but haven't yet mastered the Organization System—when a major piece looms, return to these sections for guidance. Master the system—it works for every kind of writing and speaking. Then vary it and create new structures or approaches.

9

ADDRESSING YOUR PUBLIC

Given the choice of speaking in public or boiling in oil, most people would choose olive.
                                                              —Phyllis Mindell

Whatever your heart holds, whatever your promise, whatever your good ideas, you must know how to get the story out in a shape that audiences not only understand but accept. Every speaking encounter, whether with one individual across a desk or one million across a cable, acts as a trial to test your leadership capacity. This chapter challenges you to synthesize what you've learned so far in various situations, offers Do it Now! ideas to help you succeed, and gives How to Say It exact words for support.

Speaking to Large Audiences

Invariably, the executive chair heats up—you have to address large audiences. But now you're not just you anymore—you're Company A. If you ramble and look disorganized, Company A looks disorganized. And it's no longer just *your* story that you relate; it's the story of the division or company or group. Discard the casual, the spontaneous, the unplanned talk (it can look casual or spontaneous, but only if you plan well)—this is the big time. And this is the time to establish your (and your company's) credibility.

My executive clients usually call when they face their first major speech. Public speaking serves as a crucible for leadership communications. This section tells sad stories of public speaking disasters (the stories are true but camouflaged to avoid embarrassment). Next, we walk through the Organization System for an actual presentation or talk, the kind you may be called upon to deliver one day soon. Finally, we detail the preparations for a smooth, successful talk or presentation.

THE STORIES

The trusted division president was to speak to young fast-track employees in his own division. Their future lay in his hands. Before he entered, the room hushed and all eyes turned to the entrance. He strode in, a dashing figure, well-dressed and well-groomed. He took his place at the front of the room and managed to stand between the projector and the screen, unintentionally casting his shadow behind him. He soon realized this and moved out of the way. Speaking without notes, he began his hesitations almost immediately: "um" and "uh" punctuated his comments. He relied on slides prepared by consultants. The slides hindered his performance: the bullets weren't in parallel and couldn't be delivered as if they were sentences, yet they prevented him from speaking spontaneously. He showed a short training video and announced, "If you don't watch this video at least seven times, you won't succeed." This was the first of several threats starting with the phrase, "If you don't . . ."

As the talk progressed, his confidence waned and the audience began to drift away. Where, at the start, everyone sat straight and attentive, they gradually slipped down into their seats and began to slouch or doodle (no side conversations took place—after all, this was the boss). By the end of the talk, gloom prevailed. Six months later, the division president was replaced.

She strode into the room. The new president had chosen appropriate trappings and carried herself proudly at this first presentation for a woman's professional group at her new firm. The strong nonverbal skills couldn't balance the weak use of language. Nearly every sentence began with an "I" followed by "think," "feel," or "believe." And her "sort of" undermined fifteen statements; for example, "We'll sort of revamp the marketing department." She never mentioned the name of the group whom she addressed or any individuals in it. At the reception afterward, remarks like, "I won't follow her anywhere" filled the room. Her tenure lasted less than a year. My files (and your heads) contain hundreds of examples of failures like these, failures made by competent and intelligent strategists who failed to lead because they failed to get people to follow. And they could not get people to follow because they neglected to plan or practice.

Planning a Presentation

Let's see what they might have done. We'll walk through the thirteen steps for a typical, crucial presentation: the opportunity to meet the group you're about to lead.

STEP 1 THINK ABOUT THE AUDIENCE.

Learn about the audience, even if you're asked to speak about yourself. Our hypothetical talk is our first before the fast-track young people ending a week of training. Informal inquiry reveals that they were hand-picked for their promise. Most have worked for the company fewer than three years. They come from five different countries; 60 percent are men; 30 percent represent minority populations. Their backgrounds are in engineering, finance, and marketing. By all accounts they are enthusiastic about this opportunity.

STEP 2 DETERMINE THE PURPOSE.

This is not a report, a board session, or a speech to strangers. Others have given the training sessions. You aim to *welcome them to the new e-marketing program*, *inspire them to fulfill the ambitious targets you've set, and foster creative approaches in a new endeavor*. Note that each purpose opens with a verb and completes the verb phrase.

STEP 3 LIST THE DETAILS.

Brain dump every detail that occurs to you, writing each on a small sticky note. Some will be deleted, some will be rephrased, all will be grouped with others to fulfill the purposes. A sampling of details follows here:

- Welcome

- Background of new group: old marketing approaches haven't worked on the Web

- Target 80 percent sales growth

- 93 percent lead generation

- 45 percent revenue increase

- What happens if they don't make it

- Rules they must follow

- Successes of telephone support program

- Examples of approaches at other firms

- Twenty other details

STEP 4   GROUP THE DETAILS.

- Welcome

- Background

- Old marketing approaches haven't worked

- Examples of approaches at other firms

- Success of telephone support program

- Targets

- 80 percent sales growth

- 93 percent lead generation

- 45 percent revenue increase

- Rules they must follow

- ~~What happens if they don't make it~~

This talk seems to have three groups of details. Note that the details could have grouped in other ways: background might fit with rules they must follow and what happens if they don't make it. As you ponder the groups, you may want to add details and remove others; for example, maybe this talk would inspire better if you don't talk about what happens if they don't make it.

STEP 5 ORDER THE DETAILS.

Within each group, decide how to sequence the details. Sequence proves an interesting challenge in all communications. For example, it might prove interesting and fun to move old marketing approaches to the end of that sequence. One possible sequence follows (yours may differ).

- Welcome

- Background

- Old marketing approaches haven't worked

- Success of telephone support program

- Examples of approaches at other firms

- Targets

- 80 percent sales growth

- 45 percent revenue increase

- 93 percent lead generation

- Rules they must follow

STEP 6 NAME THE TOPICS.

If you're working with sticky notes, mount each group onto an index card in the order you selected. Decide what to call each group. They're your topics. Write each at the top of the card.

```
┌─────────────────────────────────────────┐
│ WELCOME                                   │
└─────────────────────────────────────────┘

┌─────────────────────────────────────────┐
│ HISTORY AND BACKGROUND                    │
│ Background                                │
│ Old marketing approaches haven't worked   │
│ Success of telephone support program      │
│ Examples of approaches at other firms     │
└─────────────────────────────────────────┘

┌─────────────────────────────────────────┐
│ GOALS                                     │
│ Targets                                   │
│ 80 percent sales growth                   │
│ 45 percent revenue increase               │
│ 93 percent lead generation                │
└─────────────────────────────────────────┘

┌─────────────────────────────────────────┐
│ REMINDERS                                 │
│ Rules they must follow                    │
└─────────────────────────────────────────┘
```

STEP 7 SEQUENCE THE TOPICS.

Research shows that the order of information influences its acceptance; for example, the first and last details have the greatest likelihood of retention. Also, people accept controversial ideas more readily if the speaker has already said things they agree with. The three topics, History and Background, Goals, and Reminders have no intrinsic order: perhaps Goals should appear first in the talk, or perhaps the Reminders should be taken care of first. Look below to see the sequence this writer chose.

- Welcome

- Goals

- History and Background

- Reminders

STEP 8 WRITE THE THESIS STATEMENT.

Now that the topics and order are set, you can write the thesis statement. Just remember that the thesis statement offers a work in progress—it may change as the script emerges.

Today we challenge you with ambitious goals, fill you in on the history and background of the project, and remind you about rules the company has set.

STEP 9 WRITE THE LEAD AND END STRUCTURES.

Because the lead isn't really part of the talk, you can change it any time and tailor it to various audiences. The writer chose to lead with a lighthearted story about an e-business idea that went wrong.

Three years ago we set out to corner the xxx market by applying what we knew about marketing to e-business. Every marketer knows that human faces attract attention, so we put a talking head on our site—it sure attracted clicks but absolutely no viable leads. Your new job asks you to avoid such bloopers.

This little story lead aims to relax the audience, reduce their fear of failure, and prepare them for a difficult assignment.

The end structure may just sum up or remind listeners of that lead story:

Today you've learned the background and history of this project, heard the challenging goals you're to meet, and gotten some detail about the rules of the game. The home office will give you every support. You have our best wishes for great success. We're glad to have you aboard. Thanks.

STEP 10 PLAN THE PARAGRAPHS, TOPIC SENTENCES, TRANSITIONS, AND REMINDERS.

The beginning (lead, thesis statement) and end structures (sum up, strong end) stand ready—now build the internal logic and structure: the transitions and new topic sentences. Be sure that the lead transitions into the thesis statement.

> *What do we ask of you? We ask that you meet three goals of sales growth, revenue increase, and lead generation.*

(Details will go here)

> *To achieve these ambitious goals, please abide by the rules we've set.*

(Details will go here)

> *Now that you know what we expect and how to follow the rules, let's review the history and background of this project.*

(Details will go here)

> *In sum, today . . .*

STEP 11 WRITE THE PIECE.

Whether you plan to deliver the talk from notes, slides, an outline, or a formal script, write every word. That's the only way to ensure that the talk uses all the rhetorical and structural devices. It's also the only way to time the talk accurately: plan to write 100 words for each minute. So a fifteen-minute talk should have around 1500 words. We actually speak faster than 100 words per minute but this conservative approach allows for asides, silence, and a strong ending. No one ever complained that a talk was too short.

STEP 12 PLAN THE VISUALS (IF YOU DECIDE TO USE ANY).

At this stage, and no sooner, decide whether the speech or presentation requires visual aids. Remember that they're called *visual aids*. Most visuals hinder rather than aid talks. Still, certain kinds of information prove easier to express in a visual. For example, numerical relationships over time lend themselves to easy viewing in a graph or pie chart. If you follow the organization system and wait till the talk is written, you have a better shot at creating visuals that work. Edward Tufte's work on visuals should sit on your library shelf[27] as a guide to errors to avoid and techniques that actually convey data. He rails against poorly thought-out visuals, insisting that "slideware often reduces the analytical quality of presentations . . . in addition the popular . . . templates . . . usually weaken verbal and spatial reasoning, and almost always corrupt statistical analysis."

Tufte asserts (and experience agrees!) that the handout yields a far more effective visual aid than a projected picture. He asserts, "For serious presentations, it will often be useful to replace slides with paper handouts showing words, numbers, data, graphics, images together . . . Thoughtfully planned handouts at your talk tell the audience that you are serious and precise; that you seek to leave traces and have consequences. And that you respect your audience." Well-planned handouts also turn a presentation from a lecture to an opportunity for audience members to react and interact by jotting notes, applications, and questions on issues.

Some executives permit others to prepare packets of slides for them and then try to create cohesive talks around them—don't do it; it always fails. If you must use slides, prepare them *after* writing the text.

Also, remember that animated conversation and gestures add valuable visual aids that complement and extend oral language. They never get lost and their medium never crashes (well, hardly ever!).

STEP 13 PRACTICE, TAPE, EDIT.

This step mirrors the importance of the event. If you'll address ten people at an informal luncheon, you may not require practice and taping. But the day

---

[27]Tufte, Edward, *The Cognitive Style of PowerPoint.* Cheshire, CT: Graphics Press, 1983.

will soon come when you must speak to three thousand at an international conference—don't wing it. Learn the words, craft the moves, prepare the script (see instructions below), tape yourself, have your coach in. Your mom was right—practice does make perfect.

Do It Now!

Use the Organization System to plan and create an actual leadership talk.

10

DELIVERING SPEECHES
THAT LEAD

Don't agonize, organize.   —FLORYNCE KENNEDY

Before the Speech

The first thirteen steps have brought you along. You have a well thought-out, well-written talk with all the necessary structures and rhetorical devices, and, if necessary, the visuals. But the preparation has only begun. Now you must resolve a variety of issues to deliver that talk successfully.

PREPARE THE SCRIPT

Common wisdom and some professional speakers say, "work without scripts." Common wisdom is wrong unless you've spoken professionally. John Kennedy quipped, "Spontaneous speeches aren't worth the paper they're printed on." On paper or not, spontaneous usually fails—talks that look spontaneous or informal usually reflect hours of labor or lots of practice: blurted words rarely work. Jeff Scott Cook notes, "Most audiences would vastly prefer an interesting speech delivered from a word-for-word script to a dull and rambling speech delivered off the cuff.[28] Years of experience have yielded an ap-

---

[28]Cook, Jeff Scott, *The Elements of Speechwriting and Public Speaking.* New York: Macmillan, 1989.

proach that enables you to stick to or veer away from your script and solve most speaking problems at the same time. Simply follow those thirteen steps and prepare a full script; next set it up as described here and follow the instructions for reading aloud.

1. **Count the words in the text as a whole and in each paragraph or segment.** Estimate a speed of 100 words per minute: a one hundred word paragraph takes about a minute to deliver (calmly and with pauses and asides). If the talk is to take fifteen minutes, it should have around 1500 words.

2. **Choose a large enough, easily readable typeface (14–18 points usually works).**

3. **Set narrow top and side margins (.3"); set the bottom margin at 5.5".** Prepare a header with the name of the talk, audience, page number, and date in the upper right corner (6 point type size). Read the text aloud, marking pauses and points to stress. Craft a shorthand you recognize and use it consistently. Remember: you alone see the text—markings ease the reading task. The example below demonstrates text marking.

> (From a speech titled *Leadership in a Time of Crisis*) Fourth, leaders can be so *(make little quotation marks with fingers—hold high so everyone can see)* "nice" but so weak that they're ineffectual: //// at a board meeting last week the new director of a major university program made statements like, *(squeaky voice)* "I'm having a hard time so forgive me. I need help." And another senior person, in the mistaken belief that he was supporting the egos of his staff, said, "I really don't know anything about this subject—will you take it over, Jim." *(Pause///////////////)* Both of these managers had the right idea. They wanted to seem humble and show respect for their reports but the choice of weak language that *(lift arms high and shrink toward podium)* diminished themselves certainly won't yield the respect they seek *(lift arms wide)*. *(Take a drink of water before moving to next section.)* 109 words

4. **Isolate the end structures.** Rather then ending with the question period, save the end structures to deliver afterward. Count the words in the ending and save one extra minute (for applause or a neat finish).

5. After rehearsing and completing all markings, print the talk on card stock. Card stock is quiet, easier to handle, and more durable than paper. Decide where to place page breaks (not in the middle of a phrase or big idea). Print the word count on each page or after each paragraph. Slice the cards in half and save the blank pages (great for on-site notes and reminders—you can also list essential items such as props, pointer, business cards, clock, sticky notes, and so on). Finally, drill a hole in the upper left corner and hold all the cards together with a loose leaf ring. You'll remove the ring when delivering the talk for easy flipping of pages without drawing attention to them.

LEARN OTHER WAYS TO SCRIPT

After preparing the script, you may prefer to work from an outline or to use slides as reminders. Save these kinds of scripts till you're experienced and comfortable or for settings that do not require prepared talks. Always have a pad of sticky notes and a pen handy so you can jot down the sentence starters during question periods or other informal sessions.

READ ALOUD

People think they can't read aloud. Do you ever read to your kids? If so, or if you read in church, you have lots of experience in oral reading—simply apply the skills you already have to reading in public. Just remember the rule we mentioned earlier: **speak to people, never to the page or the screen.** Look down silently, grasp a phrase or sentence, look up, say the phrase or sentence to a person with eye contact. Look down and repeat the process. That's all there is. Make your life easier by keeping the script as high as possible on the podium; this saves you from dropping your eyes too low while glancing at the script. Of the thousands of people we've taught the skill of reading a script, only three or four failed to get the knack of it. The videotapes will tell whether you got it right.

READY THE NECESSITIES

Whether you do it yourself or a staff member does it, prepare every item you'll need on the speaker's platform. My speakers' kit carries the script, a pointer, a little clock timer, sticky notes, a pen, business cards, and any props I may want to use.

ACQUIRE THE TRAPPINGS

Consider clothing, jewelry, shoes, and hair. Many a speech has suffered because of jangling earrings, ill-fitting suits, too-short skirts, sloppy shoes, food stains, jiggling laser pointers, slippery eyeglasses, or hair that demands too much attention. One accomplished speaker described selection of a handsome two-piece silk suit. When practicing on video, she noted that the jacket lifted each time her arms rose but didn't drop when her arms dropped. Rather than tug at the top, she chose another suit. These seemingly small details matter.

MANAGE TEAM AND GROUP PRESENTATIONS

A couple of years ago, a progressive manager asked us to prepare his team for a competitive presentation. He thought the process of planning and delivering a presentation would both reward and enrich his work group. During the first run-through, we asked the group to sit as they would at the competition and we videotaped them. The tape shocked them. They sat next to each other like strangers on a bus. They never looked at each other; they didn't watch each other's talks and they passed like ships in the night as they took turns to speak.

During their class, they learned both how to present and how to work as a team. They designed an array of verbal and nonverbal signals that showed each other, and the world, that they represented a genuine, cohesive, cooperative group. For example, they told one another's accomplishments when they introduced each other. They smiled and nodded while their teammates spoke. And when one left the podium, the next shook hands with and often touched the shoulder of the other. Their long-term critique revealed that they not only presented well but that the techniques enabled them to work better daily.

If your team must present together, lead everyone to a successful performance. All the principles of individual speeches work with variations. For example, consider the whole presentation as one and each sub-presentation as a whole; then make smooth transitions from one individual to another. Team performances also yield a great benefit: You can't brag about yourself but you sure can brag about each other. Every time you say favorable words about a member of your team, you cast glory on yourself. And use everything you know about listening and body language to support the team.

CASE THE ROOM

If you've attended meetings where a participant had to pass in front of the screen to go to the bathroom, where speakers had to apologize for too-small visuals, where speakers couldn't see their own notes, where equipment failures sapped everyone's intellectual energy, you've seen what can happen when you don't case the room.

Conversely, early arrival and common sense foster success. One executive arrived early enough to look in on a session in the room in which he was to speak. This portion of the grand ballroom made a long, narrow meeting space with a rear entrance. A speaker stood, a tiny figure at the narrow front end of the room, mostly hidden by the podium and dwarfed by a huge screen. Determined not to be dwarfed, the executive asked hotel staff if the side of the room could be made its front, with the chairs arranged across the long width of the room. Because he gave plenty of notice, his request was met and his presentation was seen and heard by all.

When casing the room, check the podium. Most podiums work fine for tall people but cause problems for the short or people who must sit to speak. One of the saddest examples of bad podium fit occurred during a political convention. The keynote speaker was a young politician who promised a bright political future. The mismatch between the podium's height and hers, combined with inadequate coaching, caused millions of people to see only the tips of her fingers rather than her gestures. We never heard from her again. Success in public speaking isn't rocket science—it's good common sense.

ADJUST TO AUDIENCE SIZE

Very large audiences often watch you on a large video screen. To see how different you look, practice and tape. The video camera usually shows only the head and shoulders—adjust by raising and growing the gestures. Adjust makeup; color tends to look washed out on those large screens and skin defects show up dramatically. You won't be able to make eye contact with large audiences but do look at faces in all parts of the room.

On the Day of the Speech

Even if you case the room the day before, arrive early for your talk. Check the speaker's platform, the approach to see if it poses any problems (tripping on the way up the steps doesn't impress audiences), work with the audiovisual technician to decide where to attach the microphone if using a lavaliere (a special problem for women who wear dresses) or to adjust the sound for a fixed microphone. Decide whether your notes can wait for you on the podium while others speak.

ORGANIZE THE PODIUM

Keep the notes as high as possible; if necessary rest them atop a pad or binder. This keeps you from dropping the head each time you glance at the text. If you prefer to leave the podium or if it presents too much of a barrier, try turning it sideways where it can hold your notes and give you a handy resting place without separating you from the audience. If you want to leave the podium or work without it, you'll require a lavaliere microphone. Be sure to order it in advance. Also, place supplies such as an LED clock, a pointer, a notepad, and a water pitcher and glass in accessible spots.

ANTICIPATE PROBLEMS

Problems can come out of left field but they can also be predicted. Will this audience act friendly or angry? If you expect hostility, ask the meeting organizer to assign a moderator to protect you. Corporate audiences usually behave appropriately and rarely act crazed—that may not be true for public audiences. A business executive was invited to deliver a book review and talk at the public library. During the question period, an obviously unstable man stood to deliver a speech on a variety of unrelated topics. As he rambled, both the executive and the moderator stood paralyzed. Finally, an audience member stood up and shouted a question, silencing the tirade. Although you may never face such a disturbing problem, plan ahead on how to handle it if it should happen. And, if you have a moderator, be sure the moderator understands that he or she must actually moderate.

Do you expect hostile or difficult questions? Can you tolerate interruptions or questions during the talk? If not, let people know that they should hold questions till the end or request that questions be written on cards and passed up front. But all the anticipating in the world won't prevent surprises—handle them calmly and your authority will prevail.

WELCOME AND LEARN

You arrived early enough to set up—now take a place at the entrance or walk from person to person. Introduce yourself as the speaker and ask individuals a relevant question. Have you had experience with e-business marketing? Has public speaking posed problems for you? What company are you with? Keep a notepad or blank cards handy—the replies can enrich the speech and make it personal. And the fact that you showed interest in people ensures that they'll show interest in you when you speak.

WATCH THE CLOCK

Set the count-down timer and turn it on as you say the first word. If you've scripted well, you'll meet the time requirements but questions or asides can consume minutes and you must end on time. You could keep an eye on the clock in the room (never look at a wristwatch during a presentation) but that adds complexity to a complex challenge. Or an aide in the audience can remind you when the end nears. However you manage it, end on time.

HANDLE TIMING CHANGES

You may be asked to shorten your talk by fifteen minutes or more. Do not panic. Your talk has a strong beginning and end and well-constructed interior structures. Simply omit some of the interior structures, remove them from the thesis statement, and deliver the talk on time and with confidence.

DELIVER

Your work is done. Now relax and enjoy the speech—your audience will forgive (or more likely, not notice) errors if you seem to enjoy yourself. Your audience will stiffen if you look terrified. Remember to pay close attention to the listeners. Don't worry whether you're doing a good job but do worry about the audience's comfort. It's okay to raise your hand (to demonstrate that they should raise theirs) and ask, "Can everyone hear?" "Can you all see?"

END WELL

Count the words in the strong ending and save enough time to deliver it after the question period, enabling you to end gloriously rather than say, "If there are no more questions, I guess we're done." Whatever you do don't heave a sigh and run off the stage. If people clap at the end, smile and enjoy it or applaud for them.

After the Speech

Review every performance. Learn both failure and success analysis. Once a year, tape a major speech. Send the audio to the transcription service and review every word. Did you stay close to the script? Did the speech's organization reveal itself clearly enough? Did the "I" statements and other weak forms take a low percent of the total words? Did you use all the structural and rhetorical devices? Do action verbs drive most sentences? Use the checklists in this book as a standard and make sure each talk is better than the one before.

Next, turn the voice off and view the nonverbal communications. Again, you should look more poised, authoritative and confident each time you speak.

If the speech was especially well-received, ask why. Was it the words, the gestures, or the great fit between you and the audience? Can you repeat or reuse the best elements? If audience critiques are available, read them in detail—they often contain useful suggestions and ideas.

You've now walked through the entire process of speech creation from idea to performance. As your career advances, you'll stand ready to meet each new challenge with vigor and enthusiasm and your message will go out to the world.

But most of your presentations aren't for large audiences—they're for individuals and small groups.

11

COMMUNICATING WITH SMALL GROUPS AND INDIVIDUALS

The vast preponderance of personal leadership is exerted quietly
and subtly in everyday relationships. —JAMES MACGREGOR BURNS

In *Leadership*[29] James MacGregor Burns notes, "The vast preponderance of personal leadership is exerted quietly and subtly in everyday relationships." Those everyday relationships enable you to forge the bonds that strengthen yourself and those whom you would lead. Every time you lead a meeting, negotiate an agreement, engage in an argument, or meet an employee, the language of leadership drives your success. This chapter extends the principles and language ideas to help you lead in everyday situations.

Meetings That Work

Even professional speakers talk mainly in informal conversation at meetings, conferences, and small presentations. Yet the informality of a situation doesn't provide an excuse for sloppy, mindless, or out-of-control language. Before meetings, prepare: select the environment, consider problem people, weigh the

---

[29]Burns, James MacGregor, *Leadership*. New York: Harper and Row, 1978.

possibility of hostile or argumentative conversations (you can usually predict them), and use your language knowledge to prepare How to Say It notes.

SELECT THE ENVIRONMENT AND TRAPPINGS

Space matters, room temperature matters, food matters, your location matters, comfort matters. Wise choices enable you to get your ideas across and listen effectively to others. Consider whether to sit or stand: height yields power; it also can make you easier to see. If asserting control, stand at the head of the table or front of the room. If sharing control, sit in a middle position at the table. In general the closer you stand to other people, the easier it is to connect with them. The notions of presence and charisma apply at small meetings just as they apply with large audiences: leaders perceived as charismatic stay close to people and touch them.

CHECKLIST FOR MEETING ENVIRONMENT

- ❑ Space
- ❑ Seating
- ❑ Temperature
- ❑ Lighting
- ❑ Refreshments
- ❑ Position
- ❑ Props

FOSTER PARTICIPATION

Your language and behavior foster or discourage participation. Acquire a repertoire of sentences that do both. Here are models of How to Say It:

SENTENCES THAT ENCOURAGE PARTICIPATION

- *Thanks for a creative idea.*

- *That could work.*

- *Bill, please comment on your reaction.*

- *Danita, please describe your group's experience.*

- *Ramon, will that work?*

- *Tom, you have expertise in that—what do you think about it?*

SENTENCES THAT DISCOURAGE PARTICIPATION

- *That may prove important, but it's not on the agenda for today.*

- *Thanks—could you hold those comments till the end?*

- *Please hold comments till the end.*

WELCOME PEOPLE. ASSERT AUTHORITY BY CREDITING THEIR ACCOMPLISHMENTS

- *Before we begin, thanks, Jill, for preparing the budget. The clarity and accuracy of the graphs ease our job today.*

- *Thanks to all of you for traveling long distances to be here today. We'll make every effort to make it worth your while.*

- *Kudos to all of you for a job well done.*

- *A big security problem looms; we must figure out how to deal with it. Your skills and background—Jim's government security, Sam's years at the FBI, Ali's experience with equipment—will help resolve this issue.*

Notice how few "I" statements appear and how many "please" and "thanks" do. That's the civil discourse that builds teams, grows morale, and sets the stage for necessary and civil disagreement.

PREPARE FOR DIFFICULT OR HOSTILE PEOPLE

Every group brings one or more difficult, hostile, or confrontational people. Meeting problems are predictable if you know the people in the group. Prepare to reassert your authority by managing bad behavior. Few people act obnoxious to the one in the executive suite; they reserve their hostility for the young and the weak, whom you must protect.

SEVEN APPROACHES TO DIFFICULT PEOPLE

1. **Public humiliation fails.** Speak privately: *Foul language demoralizes everyone. Please hold your tongue at meetings.*

2. **Keep notes, accumulate evidence.** *The meeting transcript shows that you interrupt nearly every time Sal speaks. These interruptions diminish her in everyone else's eyes. Please let her finish her comments.*

3. **Ease hostility with passive constructions.** *Behavior like that won't be tolerated (accepted, welcomed, approved).*

4. **Force civility.** If necessary, open the meeting with a statement like: *Some of our meetings have been disrupted by cursing and uncivil behavior. That simply won't be tolerated. If things get out of hand, people will be asked to leave.*

5. **Protect the weak.** *Constantly interrupting other people makes it impossible for them to get their ideas across. Please let him finish his presentation.*

6. **Use timers when appropriate.** Aggressive people may try to monopolize discussion; as leader, you must exercise control. An easy way of doing so is insisting that no one takes more than a certain number of minutes.

7. **Ask people to write their comments on index cards.** The moderator can choose which comments to read.

ARGUE EFFECTIVELY

Consultants who attend meetings in the United States and abroad comment on Americans' unwillingness to argue. Because we lack ways to disagree civilly, we fear any expression of doubt or disagreement. So we tend to fall into "group speak," in which everyone knows the team is making the wrong decision but no one knows how to say so. Hans Christian Anderson's story "The Emperor's New Clothes" says it perfectly: the thieves who pretended to weave a golden suit for the emperor intimidated everyone into agreeing that they indeed had woven a golden garment. It wasn't until a child at the parade announced that the emperor had no clothes on that everyone admitted the truth. Well, you must encourage those who see the truth to speak it even when they disagree with everyone else, even you.

An article titled "How Management Teams Can Have a Good Fight"[30] describes a study comparing management teams working under high pressure. Researchers found that those who collaborated most successfully also engaged in the most vigorous argument, but avoided interpersonal hostility, politicking, and posturing. They used the same six tactics for managing conflict: they debated on the basis of facts, developed multiple alternatives, shared commonly agreed-upon goals, injected humor into the decision process, maintained a balanced power structure, and resolved issues without forcing consensus (they called it *consensus with qualification*). The authors write: "Reasonable people, making decisions under conditions of uncertainty, are likely to have honest disagreements over the best path for their company's future. Management teams whose members challenge one another's thinking develop a more complete understanding of the choices, create a richer range of options, and ultimately make . . . effective decisions. . . ."

How, then, can the language of leadership promote successful argument? First, set the ground rules: avoid "I" statements (this alone elevates discourse); speak about subjects, not people; maintain civility; listen deeply; avoid hostile interruptions; laugh but not at each other; seek consensus but be ready to make decisions in its absence.

---

[30]Eisenhardt, Kathleen M., Jean L. Kahwajy and L.J. Bourgeois, "How Management Teams Can Have a Good Fight," *Harvard Business Review* (July-August 1997), pp. 77–85.

Do It Now!

If your team or management group fails to argue successfully and civilly, have a videotape and transcript made of a meeting. Distribute it to all team members so they can analyze what each said and whether it worked. Teach the principles of civil argument and make another tape. Ask each individual to measure changes he or she made. Transcript analysis reveals change vividly.

Leading One Person at a Time

Think about a typical week. How many one-to-one encounters do you have? In what circumstances? Congratulating people for jobs well done; chastising them for failures; mentioning future leaders; inspiring them to a goal; delivering critiques; or myriad other circumstances.

Do It Now!

You'll find below actual encounters typical of those executives must manage every day. For each, note structures (how to begin, when to include difficult material, how long meeting should take, how to end, how to record what happened), trappings, nonverbal behaviors, and words you'd use if the event took place in your office. Use all the information you've learned so far.

A dreadful earnings report came in from the finance department, whose head you must meet.

Structures

_____

_____

Trappings

_____

_____

Nonverbal

_____

_____

Words

_____

_____

The young engineer has earned a major promotion.

Structures

_____

_____

Trappings

_____

_____

Nonverbal

_____

_____

Words

_____

_____

A board member has written a nasty letter about your performance and requested to see you.

Structures

_____

_____

Trappings

_____

_____

Nonverbal

_____

_____

Words

_____

_____

Do It Now!

Describe a difficult situation you will face in the executive suite and plan the
scenario on the lines below.

Situation

_____

Structures

_____

_____

Trappings

_____

_____

Nonverbal

_____

_____

_____

Words

_____

_____

_____

Delivering Critiques

My company gives presentation skills seminars for people from nearly every country and at various management levels. These popular classes are known (lovingly) as "seminars from hell" not only because we videotape and offer detailed critiques but because each participant must deliver a formal critique to a peer. Yet, despite the anxiety inherent in the course, after three days people speak of the group as "family" and exchange addresses so they can keep in touch. And months and years later, they report that the language of critique proved the most valuable aspect of the course. You address large audiences once in a while but you deliver critiques every day in the executive suite.

Yet the language of critique does no more than apply all the ideas you've read here. The secret is that it's neither about us nor about you—it's about the behavior and the words.

HOW TO SAY IT IN CRITIQUE

1. Remember body language. If your eyes fail to touch those of the listener, your credibility, good will or confidence will be doubted. Open the body, smile at the recipient (when appropriate), make eye contact, listen carefully, and keep accurate notes—these silent ways deliver the only caring language of critique.

2. Omit touchy-feely words. Critique shouldn't harbor weak utterances such as, "I liked it," "Great," "You did a good job." Choose precise words—they're the only route to loving critique.

3. Talk about products, processes, and behaviors, not about yourself or the listener. Sentences like, "Your work surpassed all the benchmarks," "The design exceeded the client's expectations," "The report arrived late and failed to address the client's expectations," meet the highest standards for a caring language of critique. They also yield a neutral language that delivers both positive and negative critiques without rancor or hostility.

4. Refer to the recipient by name. It shows your genuine interest.

5. Prefer action verbs. Work succeeds or fails because of what it does or doesn't do, not what it is or isn't. For example, instead of "This report is really good," try, "This report shows the data concisely and clearly."

6. Use civil language, even in unpleasant situations.

7. Craft recommendations and orders precisely. "You may want to consider . . ." is a recommendation. "Please get the work in on time" is an order. Both have places in the language of critique if you and the listener know the difference. Avoid "You should . . ." and, of course, "I want you to . . ."

8. **Major critiques (for example, annual employee reviews and product evaluations) deserve the care and structuring of any speech: include the lead; the thesis statement; the summary; the transitions, topics and details.**

9. **Start with the strengths.** People fear critiques because they expect only the negative. "Sue, thanks for the extra support you gave the engineering group—it eased their task." "Bill, your sales increase aided our bottom line this quarter. Thanks." "Ferdinand, everyone at the office enjoys your pleasant personality, but visiting with friends on the phone during the business day distracts fellow workers."

10. **Don't presume that you know anything about the recipient's feelings or attitudes: speak only of what can be seen and documented.** Rather than, "You felt confident," say "You appeared confident," or "The smooth blend of verbal and nonverbal made you seem confident."

11. **Encourage and allow time for the recipient to respond and add insights and information.** If necessary, ask leading questions, "Don, what's your perception of the problem?" "Amina, what's your reaction to these suggestions?" "Does this consequence seem fair?"

Do It Now!

Craft the skeleton of a detailed critique of a person's job performance or a piece of work. Include a lead, thesis statement, strong end structures, internal transitions and topics.

Negotiating

Negotiating is both strategic and linguistic: what is said and done at the negotiation affects the possibility of reaching strategic goals. For the communication aspect of negotiations, let's revisit the principles laid out by the social psychologist Robert Cialdini and see how these can improve negotiating sessions.

Liking

The liking principle states that one will be more persuasive if he or she is either liked or seen as cooperative, attractive, or similar or pays legitimate compliments to the negotiating partner. By this principle, comments like the following can ease negotiations: "Time has shown that we share the goal of a satisfying and successful relationship between labor and management," "Ricardo, thanks for taking the trouble to get here from Omaha today. Did you know that I also grew up in Omaha and went to Nebraska State?" "What stunning earrings!"

Authority

People are more easily influenced by those they perceive to be legitimate authorities. You can establish authority with handouts that list previous experience in similar situations or mention them casually early in the session. Cialdini also suggests that you win respect by acknowledging the merit of the other side's case.

Scarcity

Research on this principle has "demonstrated that, in situations characterized by uncertainty, presenting . . . what stands to be lost by a failure to take action is more persuasive than emphasizing what is to be gained by taking the action." Thus, you might note that they'd lose the opportunity to design a resolution tailored specifically to their needs and interests. "This is our only opportunity to work it out face to face."

Consistency

To make the most of consistency avoid having parties state their "bottom line" positions but rather to "specify their underlying interests and agree publicly to consider a wide range of options." Be sure everyone agrees to the commitment orally and in writing.

Reciprocity

You "can increase the likelihood that the other side will adopt a collaborative approach if you are courteous and forthcoming rather than combative and uncooperative."

Citation

People in uncertainty want to know what others did. You can point to typical settlements in similar situations or note the types of provisions that have worked in similar cases.

As always, open body language, eye contact, touch, civility, and kindness position you to negotiate successfully.

Nurturing Leadership

In our view, *mentor* signifies such deep understanding of a skill that one is capable of passing it on to others and building succession. We have known masters who could not grow to mentor others: when they moved on, the groups they led failed to prosper. Others look to the future as they mentor and nurture future leaders. To some, the very definition of leadership includes developing new leaders and planning succession.

Howard Gardner and others have listed early characteristics of future leaders, including high energy level, ability to perform under pressure, desire to win, willingness to make sacrifices to accomplish goals, comfort with risk, and, always, exceptional communication skills. Novice leaders also show a willingness to confront those in power—don't pick sycophants, even if they feed your ego. How, then, can you apply *How to Say It for Executives* to foster future leaders?

First, seek to provide novice leaders with *educative* opportunities. John Dewey spoke of "educative conditions" that enhance future experiences; he contrasted these with "miseducative" experiences that have the effect of arresting or distorting future growth. "Just as no man lives or dies to himself, so no experience lives or dies to itself. . . . Every experience lives on in further experiences." As mentor, you bear the responsibility of determining which opportunities have the best chance of living on to enrich the future of the fledgling leader. An example comes to mind of the graduate student in whom mentors saw promise. Because the student's peers live all over the world, the mentors funded a semester of teaching and research abroad. This proved both a test and an educative experience: the student both demonstrated and enhanced his ability to work with others, teach in a different environment, and forge links to a global network. Contrast that with what happened to many young dot-commers who lived through rapid but fleeting moments of un-earned wealth and emerged weakened and disillusioned—they suffered a miseducative experience that lived on to sour future experiences.

The suggestions in this section refer to communication skills; novices and apprentices also require help with relevant financial, strategic, and organiza-tional attributes.

1. Offer public speaking opportunities. Every beginning speaker errs—novices and apprentices learn early from their errors and prepare them-selves for their next speaking challenges. For example, if you're to be out of town on the date of a speaking invitation, offer to send the mentee. Alert fledgling speakers to public speaking techniques you've found use-ful. Guidance of a wise elder proves faster and less traumatic than painful experience.

2. Encourage the future leader to critique your work. A senior executive routinely requests critiques from his mentees when he speaks in public. One observed that he tended to tap his foot when addressing factory work-ers but not when addressing peers.

3. Make opportunities for future leaders to organize and run meetings.

4. Share your own experiences. Here's one of the few occasions where it's both acceptable and desirable to talk about yourself. "I had the same prob-lem the first time I got up to speak to an audience. . . ."

5. Have videos and transcripts made of the future leader speaking, sitting at a meeting, and running a meeting. Ask him or her to craft a critique.

6. Hold the fledgling leader to the highest standards.

7. Show belief in the fledgling. When Shirley Tilghman, president of Princeton, was a young scientist, she found no female role models who were also mothers. But she did find a mentor, Phil Leder, "a very success-ful scientist." When she asked him if women could make the kind of com-mitment it took to succeed in science and mothering, he said, "Don't be ridiculous. There's no reason why you can't do both of these things."[31] That kind of belief spurs potential leaders and inspires them to strive.

Do It Now!

Review your approach to shaping leaders. List ways to improve it.

Leadership in a Time of Crisis: When Inspiration Matters Most

Crises temper leaders. Those we remember lovingly proved capable of uttering words that comforted or uplifted us during difficult times. And the best of these model words and behavior we can emulate during difficult times.

"Fellow citizens, we cannot escape history. We . . . will be remembered, in spite of ourselves. . . . The fiery trial through which we pass, will light us down, in honor or dishonor, to the last generation. . . . The way is plain, peaceful, generous, just, a way which, if followed, the world will forever applaud, and God must forever bless." An American president spoke these words at a time of greater danger than ours: from the windows of the White House, Abraham Lincoln watched for the approach of the South's ironclad Merrimack— the enemy was at the gates. Yet Lincoln spoke words of peace and generosity to lead the people. He stands as a model for us as we seek ways to lead during difficult times.

We all have faced and face crises in our many leadership roles: in the executive suite, the office, the shop, the classroom, and the home. Whether the crisis involved terror attacks, fear, layoffs, lost business, or children's anxiety, the exact words we say and the way we say them can ease, comfort, and inspire the people around us. We must find the humanity within us not only to endure but to endure with dignity and compassion.

---

[31]Dreifus, Claudia, "Career That Grew From an Embryo." *New York Times,* July 8, 2003.

History has shown that leaders who speak thoughtlessly, cruelly, or imprecisely can diminish and hurt both those around them and their own prospects of success, while those who speak wisely, civilly, and humanely can both comfort and inspire during difficult times.

You probably know many stories of leaders' words that failed. Think about the sources and words of those failures so you won't copy them. They usually result from absence of the language techniques covered earlier in this book. For example, the first weak language form involves constantly talking about yourself—those darned "I" statements again. A notorious failure occurred when a global company's stock began to slip. *The New York Times* published an interview with the new CEO in which he said, in essence, "You think everyone else has trouble—I lost most of my net worth." Needless to say, the stock plummeted and he soon was gone. Listen to the politicians and business people who annoy you and you'll hear loads of "I" statements.

A second failure involves imprecise use of words. A professor asked me to review a book he was completing when the country was attacked in 2001. He sought to note the relevance to the subject of his book. He wrote at a passionate time about an enormous event, but he chose words that fell short of conveying the magnitude; for example, he wrote *terrifying* when *horrific* would have proven more accurate, *hijackers* when *murderers* or *terrorists* would have conveyed the idea better, and the unfortunate phrase *different norms* when he meant *alien values*.

And, as noted earlier, President Bush's word *crusade* in the first days after the attack proved most unfortunate. Equally problematic is the word *jihad,* whose metaphors mean vastly different things to different people.

A third source of failed leadership language involves neglect or abuse of staff. When a large clothing retailer's fortunes declined, newspapers reported that many attributed the company's difficulties to the negative and hypercritical behavior of the chief executive, who publicly humiliated staff members. You'll find another such example in the next chapter; a CEO sent a hostile memo read by nearly everyone in the world.

Finally, leaders can be "nice," but so weak that they're ineffectual. Witness the CEO who provokes laughter in employees with the constant repetition of "sort of." And the new CEO of a Fortune 25 company whose first speech to staff was littered with dozens of "I think," "sort of," "you know," tags like "you know?" and one threat: "The company will not xxx unless the people xxx."

In contrast, successful leaders rise to crises with their language and demeanor, and we saw plenty of that during the past several years. Former Mayor Rudolph Giuliani of New York, faced with the worst crisis in American history, modeled every element of the language of leadership: he was there, he showed compassion, he spoke plainly and clearly, he did not talk about himself. No wonder the Queen of England offered him a knighthood!

And an employee told of how the CEO of one of the companies that had offices in the World Trade Center first checked that all staff had survived and then immediately emailed everyone in the firm and kept them up on developments through those awful days. Her courage and wisdom raised morale and engendered loyalty from the far flung staff of a global firm.

Tony Blair's speech before Congress in 2003, with its abundance of vivid metaphors, rhetorical power, and genuine conviction offers another model to emulate when you seek to inspire during hard times.

Let's look again at Abraham Lincoln's language in a time of crisis. Leading the country in a war of brother against brother, he always spoke with kindness and compassion, and not about himself. Look at the language of the second inaugural: "With malice toward none, with charity for all; with firmness in the right, as God gives us to see the right, let us strive on to finish the work we are in: to bind up the nation's wounds, to care for him who shall have borne the battle, and for his widow, and his orphan—to do all which may achieve and cherish a just and lasting peace, among ours, and with all nations." Here's a model for everyone in any leadership chair—next time you face a crisis, try to emulate the tone and flavor of this language.

Do It Now!

Anticipate a crisis situation you could face. Following the principles and models in this book, plan a 200–500 word talk for your staff.

12

WRITING LIKE A LEADER

The effort to write clearly compels a writer to think accurately.
—Jacques Barzun

Good news! Clear writing applies most of the skills we've already covered. Bad news! Writing poses great potential risk to your leadership authority: speak poorly and the audience knows it. Write poorly (or foolishly) and the whole world knows it.

Sad Stories

My file bulges with failed writing that leeched out to either small or huge audiences. You'll find an egregious example below, with my notes on how it failed.

A SORRY ELECTRONIC TALE

"A Stinging Office Memo Boomerangs"[32] tells of an e-mail disaster that found its way around the world, damaged the reputation of a CEO, and caused a stock to crash. A portion of the text reads, "We are getting less than forty hours of work from a large number of our . . . EMPLOYEES.

---

[32]Wrong, Edward. *The New York Times*. April 5, 2001.

The parking lot is sparsely used at 8 a.m.; likewise at 5 p.m. As managers—you either do not know what your EMPLOYEES are doing or do not CARE. You have created . . . a very unhealthy environment. In either case, you have a problem and you will fix it or I will replace you. . . . NEVER in my career have I allowed a team which worked for me to think they have a forty-hour job. I have allowed YOU to create a culture which is permitting this. NO LONGER." The executive went on to list six potential punishments. "Hell will freeze over," he vowed, before he would dole out more employee benefits. The parking lot would be his yardstick for success; it should be "substantially full at 7:30 a.m. and 6:30 p.m. You have two weeks. Tick tock."

The CEO sent the memo to four hundred recipients at his firm. It quickly took on a life of its own, was leaked, and was posted on Yahoo for worldwide circulation (and laughter). It made the rounds of the financial community and in three days the stock plummeted 22 percent.

SIX MISTAKES

1. The worst mistake was sending this message by e-mail. Analysts consulted in the article agreed, "Never try to hold large-scale discussions over e-mail. And never, ever use the company e-mail system to convey sensitive information or controversial ideas to more than a handful of trusted lieutenants." Add that nothing blurted in anger should go out till others have vetted it and you have calmed down.

2. The harsh tone of the note blunts acceptance of its message. Cool anger would have shown the writer's passion without harshness. Sentences like, "This loss of worker time threatens company growth and profit. It must be stemmed," would show how effectively the passive voice can show anger while retaining control.

3. The "I will replace you . . ." and "I allow" statements reflect an effort to dominate the readers—this may work when a general uses it in the heat of battle but fails when a modern CEO tries it. It risks loss of autonomy to its victims and will meet resistance or, at best, angry compliance.

4. The accusation that managers do not know or care may not prove correct. A question might have worked here. "Are you aware of the short hours your staff puts in?" shows the CEO's attitude without overt accusation.

5. The six threats violate the stricture, "Promise, don't threaten." A sentence like, "If profit falls as a result of low worker hours, benefits will suffer," gives the same message in a more palatable form.

6. The use of "screaming" capital letters suggests a loss of control of the medium; if you can't control your language, how can you control employees?

Let's hope none of you readers has ever scrawled a nasty memo like that one. You may be more likely to try to lead without power, as in the town supervisor's reply below. Here's the story. A town endured a debilitating ice storm; the damage took weeks to clear. A resident scrawled an angry screed that was published in the local paper. Its edited form: "To the town supervisor: I looked out my window and there is still a pile of debris. . . . I've only called the dispatcher a dozen times and . . . given up in total frustration . . . Has it dawned on you . . . that this is a problem? . . . Isn't it about time that you started running this department like a business?" (The writer goes on to describe trucks that weren't working . . .) "Did anyone in the town ever hear of outsourcing? . . . We have good equipment, we have good workers, we just don't have any supervision. The ball's in your court and let's see what you do with it."

The angry citizen obviously hasn't read this book's section on persuasion—all he did was vent but the letter caused a brouhaha in the town.

The supervisor told me of the incident and offered to show me the preliminary reply to this attack on the office. You'll find below excerpts of the original and edited version, which was published and won kudos from fellow townspeople. The words in bold show weaknesses in the first letter and changes in the second.

Original Draft Reply (excerpts)

. . . letter warrants a response that clarifies his misunderstanding based upon limited observations and partial information. **I understand** *his frustration and inconvenience, and* **I am grateful** *that his difficulties did not involve personal injuries or property loss.*

Mr. X's comments suggested a lack of understanding. . . . [the letter goes on to detail town efforts] I want to take this time to note . . . I am proud of the men and women . . . Many residents called to say how satisfied . . . I am equally appreciative of the many residents whose cooperation . . .

This letter maintains a higher tone than the complaint, but its occasional weak language makes it seem defensive and personal. Look at what a few small changes wrought.

Final Published Letter

Mr. X's letter regarding the ice storm cleanup reflects a misunderstanding based upon limited observations and partial information. An explanation is in order to clarify. . . . Consider the fact that the town . . . [the letter details work of the crews and accomplishments with no further "I" statements except one added at the end] I am proud to participate in our community.

The final letter has 25 percent fewer words, the same amount of factual information, no "I" statements (except the one added at the end), no reference to understanding the citizen's anger, and no defensive tone. It illustrates the power of language that truly leads.

The Seven Cs of Executive Writing: Navigating an Incredible Journey

The sea metaphor comes naturally to those who lead: most of us feel as though we're drowning in a sea of words when we write. Yet, although writing takes us on an incredible journey toward a distant and seemingly unreachable shore, it can prove a journey of discovery—of our audiences, of our pursuit of the truth, of our ideas, even of ourselves. Everything you've learned so far comes to fruition when you write. You don't have to learn many new ideas, but you do have to apply what you know in a new context.

To launch your writing journey, we'll skim the surface of clear writing in the executive suite by visiting seven buoys that can mark our way: community, content, complexity, control, clarity, compression, and continuity. After a brief overview of each issue, we'll cite examples from current professional writing as well as from my fancy.

You'll get suggestions not only for clear professional writing but for e-mail that doesn't sink faster than the *Titanic*.

1. COMMUNITY

Leaders may spend days alone but corporate life advances as a communal event. Executives' writings must converge and synthesize with the work of others on their teams, in their offices, and around the world. Before embarking on a piece of writing, the writer always asks, who will read this? Do you write only for engineers on your team or do you expect marketing executives to read the work as well? Do your customers live locally or do they dwell in far-flung locations? Are they native speakers or are they struggling to understand a second or third language?

Failure to deal with this issue of audience leads executives to distance themselves from those in other disciplines as well as from others who should understand what they do. Therefore, learn to traverse the boundaries that separate you from the many audiences you wish to reach. Also, keep the audience's expectations in mind when writing—that's what community means: reaching out to convey ideas in a form the audience will find readable and understandable.

Do It Now!

When you get back to work, print out a few recent pieces of yours and ask if you considered community as you wrote: community requirements, community interests, even community language.

Once you take community into account, you must select the content. The Organization System and Goldilocks principle help: include just the right content to support the thesis, not too much and not too little.

2. CONTENT

Content goes beyond content of the piece. It also addresses content of each sentence. We can use sentence forms that load up lots of content, but the content must be related. The sentence that follows has very simple content expressed in the most complex way.

> *The anomalous result of the processes, which were conducted at the National Research Labs in Bethesda, Maryland, in the northeastern quadrant of the United States by a remanufacturing team consisting of one senior engineer and six empowered lab technicians and in conjunction with studies done in France as well as studies done in Italy by a team of engineers from the Soviet Union and which were analyzed on the DMB computer program located at the central site in Transylvania and transmitted by data satellite to the various sites, appeared to be an artifact of the different languages spoken by the researchers.*

Contrast that to the sentence below, which contains complex content expressed in a simple way.

> *This confusion results from the differences in languages at the various sites.*

3. COMPLEXITY

Strive not for simplicity but for clarity in writing. Indeed, good writing accepts, even welcomes, complexity as it seeks to convey difficult ideas. Still, executives seem to take the notion of complexity as a grammatical rather than as a conceptual one: they write as many complex and convoluted sentences as possible. They haven't figured out yet that complex ideas can reach full expression in simple language. To welcome and express complexity, first separate the notions of complex ideas and complex sentences—the first we want; the second we respect (and our readers fear).

Here is a simple sentence that expresses a complex idea:

The change served as a marker of future changes.

Here is an overly complicated sentence that expresses a relatively simple idea:

In the customer's factory which was visited by the field engineer, the copier was found to be located in the parameters of the liquid runoff, implying that the increased hazard is due to post-manufacture leakage, most likely from the periphery, through either the vacuum suction tubes or random movement of excess factory personnel, or through other factors regulating the temperature of the runoff, which causes reduced temperature at the location of the foreman station, which is near the coffee machine that tends to leak while the coffee is brewing.

Here is a simple sentence that conveys profoundly complex ideas:

Through the text, the reader becomes a writer. (Helen Vendler)

Einstein said, "Make things as simple as possible, but no simpler." Welcome and embrace complexity in your writing. Just remember to express complexity as clearly and simply as possible. A commitment to complexity in thought should not link to a commitment to complexity in writing.

How to Say It

- Limit most sentences to one independent and one dependent clause.
- Limit the number of prepositional phrases in any one sentence.
- Express complexity through precise noun and verb choices.
- Show relationships through parallelism.

4. CONTROL

Just as the navigator and the captain must control the vessel through the shoals of language, the writer must control and coordinate all the many elements of written language: the word, the phrase, the clause, the sentence, the paragraph, the punctuation, and so on. Losing control over any one element hinders the full expression of ideas.

One element that poses problems for executive writers is punctuation. We rarely think about punctuation, yet its use can illuminate or cloud meaning.

Here is an example in which out-of-control commas reverse the meaning of the sentence:

> *Executives who assert that gold fillings send messages to your brain also assert that Martians landed last year.*

Fortunately, few executives would count themselves among that group. Now see what happens when we add two little commas:

> *Executives, who assert that gold fillings send messages, also assert that Martians landed last year.*

Now the sentence suggests that *all* executives make these dubious assertions. The writer better check his or her gold fillings!

A small change in punctuation can change the meanings in still another way:

> *"Executives" who assert that gold fillings send messages also assert that Martians landed last year.*

The addition of the quotation marks around "executives" shows the author's disdain for the claimants, suggesting that only fake executives make such silly assertions.

How to Say It

Gain control through use of the grammar checker and keep good references on hand to avoid silly errors. If good fortune brings you a superb administrative aide who knows language, he or she can offer suggestions. And don't hesitate to use outside editors, coworkers, and colleagues to give the reader's perspective.

5. CLARITY

Clarity results from the blending of all the elements we've discussed so far: community, complexity, content, and control. Clarity seems a distant vision, a lovely island shrouded in fog, but it's actually no more than the product of careful thought and coordination.

A group of professors at a medical school asked for review of a letter to senior management requesting a change in hiring and promotion of women. The letter noted, "At the school, women hold very few senior positions." "Very few" offers vague information—how many is very few? 3, 10, 1 percent? Well, it turns out that the word should have been "no," as in "none." The edited sentence reads, "At the school, women hold no senior positions." What a difference clarity makes!

Clarity also reflects careful choice of the medium of information, and it can save or destroy life itself. Edward Tufte in *Visual and Statistical Thinking* tells the terrible tale of the Challenger failure and attributes it to the engineers' failure, through charts, to persuade management not to launch. He writes, "The selection of data—whether partisan, hurried, haphazard, uninformed, thoughtful, wise, can make all the difference. . . . The chart makers had the correct theory and they were thinking causally, but they were not *displaying* causally." Tufte goes on to show how a scatterplot would have shown the danger of low temperatures. He says, "In the thirteen charts . . . there is a scandalous discrepancy between the intellectual tasks at hand and the images created to serve those tasks . . . there are right ways and wrong ways to show data; there are displays that reveal the truth and displays that do not." He shows the damage of what he calls *chartjunk* and says, "Clear and precise seeing becomes as one with clear and precise thinking. . . . It also helps to have an endless commitment to finding, telling, and showing the truth." Clear writers link clear and precise thinking with clear and precise expression, both verbally and visually.

Do It Now!

Ask someone from another field (or one of your children) to read your words and illustrations and tell you if they make sense. If they say, as my nine-year-old said to me when I was in graduate school, "This sounds like psychology mumbo-jumbo," it probably is and you must go back to the drawing board.

How to Say It

Force clarity by preferring action verbs. To the extent that you can tell what people and things *do* you can attain clarity.

Let's look at a few examples.

The meeting was held at the facility and the new project was discussed but agreement was not reached and it was agreed that another meeting should be held.

Let's see what this poor writer tried to say:

Our discussion of the new project failed to yield agreement and we plan to meet again.

6. COMPRESSION

If our destination is a distant but visible shore an hour away, we surely don't want to do what Columbus tried to do: we want to attain west by sailing west, not east and coming back. Compression enables us to reach our shore as quickly and efficiently as possible. Tools of compression (and of course of clarity, complexity, and community as well) include most of the topics we've covered but they also include the advanced grammar forms that empower us to say what we must say in as few words as possible. Parallelism, the most powerful spoken form, proves equally powerful in writing.

Do It Now!

Write a parallel list of what you've learned so far in this book.

_____

_____

_____

_____

How to Say It

Learn parallelism and use it as much as possible. The few moments you invest in casting ideas in parallel will cut the length of your written documents, add to their clarity and vigor, and save your readers hours—thus earning their gratitude and admiration.

7. CONTINUITY

You know the familiar elements of continuity in the piece as a whole: headings, Roman numerals, enumeration. But remember the value of continuity within and between sentences. Tools of continuity include words whose meanings are known to you, but perhaps you never learned to love them as the wind that drives the sails of your writing:

- Tools that chart the course: *first, second, third; next, after*

- Tools that build the argument: *also, in addition, moreover, all of these*

- Tools that take exception: *yet, still, although, despite, however*

- Tools that summarize: *all in all, in sum, in summary, in a nutshell, to sum up*

These tools, known to all of you, placed carefully, yield logic and fluency that takes the reader smoothly from one idea to the next, always safe from the squalls of random words and sentences that can divert the smooth course of the journey.

More Writing Pointers

TITLES

Whether for an e-mail, or a presentation, titles count. Solid titles prepare the reader for what will come and start the persuasive process.

A teacher sent an e-mail telling of a revealing experiment with titles. The same article had been published in two newspapers with two different names. It was a story about an appearance by Tom Ridge on Jay Leno's show. In one paper, the title read, "Ridge Gets the Joke, Remains Focused." The other paper's headline read, "Ridge Becoming Grist for the Humor Mill." Members of two groups received the article with one or the other headline. When quizzed on the content, the group that read the negative headline rated Ridge's performance significantly worse than the other group rated it, despite having read exactly the same article. This reminds us that persuasion (and clarity) begins with the title.

Speaking of titles, here are two e-mail tips that save your firm untold dollars. First, suggest the thesis in the headline. Instead of a headline like "Schedule," try "Finance Meeting: Jan. 12, noon, at headquarters." Next, since e-mail usually doesn't require a lead, start the message with the thesis statement. For example: "The finance committee meets on January 12 at noon at headquarters. Here's the list of information to bring."

Writing challenges our minds, our critical faculties, our creativity, our leadership ability. But if we can master the Seven Cs of executive writing, we can indeed steer our audiences and ourselves on an incredible, rich, and fulfilling journey.

Do It Now!

Community Note the communities for whom you write

_____

Jot down an example of community interests

_____

_____

Content Write a long sentence that lacks significant content

_____

_____

Write a short sentence that conveys significant content

_____

Complexity Write a complex sentence that conveys real complexity

_____

_____

Control Construct a sentence in which removal or addition of commas reverses its meaning

_____

_____

Clarity Note an instance in which poor visuals caused confusion or error

_____

Compression You'll be out of the office for a day. Write a parallel list of instructions for the temp or your secretary.

_____

_____

_____

Continuity Review a report you wrote. Add continuity as needed.

_____

Juan is a fine engineer known for his ability to manage people. He also arrives on time. In addition his quarterly budgets are met. Write a parallel sentence about him. Use any parts of speech for your parallel sequence.

_____

_____

_____

Do It Now!

PUT IT ALL TOGETHER

We've shared an incredible journey to every aspect of executive communications. Now see if you can put it all together in a piece of writing. Follow the Organization System to write one or two pages about your own language that leads. Check the Guideposts at the end of this book to be sure you include all the relevant skills. Label each in the margin (for example, lead, thesis, transition, topic sentence, internal logic, action verbs, summary, conclusion, parallel, rhetorical question, persuasion, enumeration, and so on). If you e-mail it to me, you'll get a complimentary critique.

13

BRIDGING CULTURES—TOWARD A LANGUAGE OF COMMUNITY IN A DIVERSE WORKPLACE

We meet here today not as Muslims or Christians or Jews, not as people of Arab or European descent or African or Asian descent. . . . We are children of the same God and of the same father, Abraham. We are quite literally brothers and sisters.

—JOSEPH LIEBERMAN

From Diversity to Community

In reading this book, you have learned many practical skills but, more important, you have learned a universal approach to leadership communications. This chapter extends that approach to bridge the cultural, ethnic, and racial divides that separate people in our country.

A director of a medium-sized engineering firm told about a meeting of his technical group, which comprises a right-wing Russian, a liberal Japanese, a hunter who carries rifles in his truck, and a few locals with various political views. After disagreement and vigorous argument, everyone goes to lunch together. The director, an immigrant himself, said, "This can only happen in America."

In preparing to write this chapter, I interviewed a young Chinese woman who came here for a graduate degree and now works for an American company that is sending her to start a project in China. I asked questions like, "What mistakes have you seen made at meetings?" and "What should Americans avoid in diverse workplaces?" Her replies stressed her positive experiences. "My bosses here give me words of encouragement; in China the bosses gave only negative words." "Americans promote people based on performance; in China it's connections." My informant returns to China aiming to make her workplace there more like an American workplace. We have the best of diverse workplaces. Sometimes, however, we fall short.

We fall short when we make the way hard for expatriates and immigrants. A French executive who spent a few years in the United States told of language mix-ups that could have cost him his job, and that alienated him. For example, in France sexual bantering is an accepted part of work life, but when he made a small sexual joke in the United States, he was accused of harassment. When he used the standard French term *Afrique Noir,* he was accused of racism. But he also complained that Americans act friendly but are not, telling of a manager who said, "You and your wife will have to come to a barbecue at our house." The Frenchman believed he had been invited but no date was ever set and no true invitation extended.

Whatever other barriers divide us, language, both verbal and nonverbal, can bring us together—not just good intentions, not just kind hearts, not just understanding but specific measurable changes in our behaviors. Diversity can tear us apart or enrich our lives; it can create a workplace of factions or one of community; it can cost dearly in lost productivity or add richly to growth. If we seek to shape an environment in which diversity enriches and broadens our lives and our companies, we must go far beyond "understanding" differences: we must change old behaviors that no longer work.

We must learn to listen critically to our own language as leaders; shed the words, sentences, and gestures that alienate others; and acquire the words, sentences, and gestures that engage others. We must learn *the language of community*. Small changes, easily understood and applied, can head off large resentments and go far toward transforming "diversity" into "community" at work.

Many years of experience with people in and from nearly every country and with every kind of background generated the language forms that you have already learned in this book. It turns out that they also bridge the chasms that separate people, chasms of gender, of age, of education, of race, of nationality, of gesture, of class, of word choice. If you apply and extend the principles of *How to Say It for Executives* you can transform your diverse work environment into a true community in which people work more civilly, more generously, and more productively.

Language that Breeds Animosity

Let's look at language that leads to animosity and see how to transform it. Each was actually said (or done) by an executive. Check the items that you've heard or said at your work place.

- ☐ *She's a fine manager and yet she remains a woman.*

- ☐ *She's not very attractive but she's a good scientist.*

- ☐ *You always look so pretty.*

- ☐ *You people always do that.*

- ☐ *People from that country smell funny so I don't like to work with them.*

- ☐ *Did you hear the story about the fox and the dog?*

- ☐ *When I got the award, the manager shook hands with the (white) guy before me but gave me a high five. I was insulted.*

Take another look at these sentences and behaviors. They share two common traits: they treat people as members of a group rather than as individuals and they assume that personal characteristics have something to do with work. *She's a fine manager and yet she remains a woman* and *She's not very attractive but she's a good scientist* assume there's incompatibility between being a woman and being a manager or a scientist. *You always look so pretty* can be viewed as harassment but even if it's just a compliment it has nothing to do with work or merit (unless the recipient is a model). *You people always do that* and *People from that country smell funny so I don't like to work with them* assume that everyone with a particular background is exactly like everyone else with that background (the source of most hatreds in the world today). *Did you hear the story about the fox and the dog?* opens an offensive joke (beware of jokes—most offend someone).

When I got the award, the manager shook hands with the (white) guy before me but gave me a high five. I was insulted. This was spoken by the recipient of inappropriate behavior: the manager assumed that you shake the hands of white engineers but you give a high five to black engineers. In every case, the manager involved meant no harm but did harm nonetheless.

Had the people who generated these inappropriate words and gestures learned the principles detailed in this book, they'd have avoided these unpleasant and damaging failures.

VERBAL PRINCIPLES FOR A LANGUAGE OF COMMUNITY

We can start to build bridges between people by following a few simple principles. First, talk about work rather than people. Had the sentences above done so, they'd have said, *She's a fine manager* or *a good scientist* or *You always get here on time* or *That behavior is unacceptable* or *Some people are allergic to certain perfumes.*

Second, avoid emotional words and embrace precise, civil language. On first glance, these ideas may seem contrary to community-building. Wouldn't we work better if we talk about how much we like each other and how good we feel about each other? That's the premise that spreads the infection of touchy-feely language at work—and can lead to ugly personal confrontation. Think about disagreements at meetings: "I feel that this is a good idea. I feel that it's a bad idea. I disagree. You're wrong. I like this idea. I feel good about this project. You people always come late. They never get their work done right."

Our Well-Read seminars attract professionals and workers from nearly every country, complexion, and background, and we tell them what could be painful truths about the way they speak, write, lead, listen, and give presentations. Yet they accept, even welcome, our critiques. Why? Because we never talk about ourselves or about them. We can say negative things about a person's writing or the way he or she walks to the podium to speak. Comments such as, "This piece has no thesis statement; Reading from the screen bores the audience; Jingling earrings detract from the message; Turning the back to the audience loses its attention," earn warm welcomes from their victims. They offer a truly caring way to lead and influence people . . . and to build bridges.

Another caveat here: emotional words tend to address ways in which people differ. A good standard for the appropriateness of a comment is, "Would it sound strange if I said it about a white man?" So let's look at a comment like, "She's a fine manager yet she remains a woman." Would you ever say, "He's a fine manager yet he remains a man?" Even comments like, "You always look so pretty." Would you say, "You always look so handsome?" And terms like, "girl." If you call a man a "boy," them's fighting words. And when you say things like, "It's a pleasure to introduce Ellen—she always looks terrific." Would you ever say such a thing about a man in a professional setting?

Jokes, too, can harm. Any time someone says, "Some people say this joke is sexist or racist, but it's really not," better believe it is, and don't tell it. You all probably have stories of dopey jokes that insult members of the audience or their friends. Vet every joke to be sure it won't insult anyone. That's not political correctness: that's humane communications.

But we don't just want to avoid words that don't work: we must embrace words that add precision and civility to our work language. Stuart Chase, founder of Consumers' Research, said, "Words are what holds society together." As you've seen, words count: they can foster the growth of community. Choose them well and they will serve you well. Precise words reflect professionalism and objectivity. Comments like, "He always makes trouble," imply inaccurate, loose thinking, exactly what poisons the atmosphere in a diverse environment, while comments like, "On January 10, Jim said, 'I won't do this blank blank job,' " though unpleasant, are accurate and prevent accusations of unfairness or unequal treatment. Precise words enable us to show fairness and treat people equally, whatever their background, race, age, or ethnicity.

"But," the Roman poet Horace said, "words once spoke can never be recalled." This brings us to the value of civility in harvesting community from the seeds of diversity. Simple words like "please" and "thank you," thoughtful words, kind words pay off immeasurably. Curses, slurs, insults, once spoken, can never be recalled. They poison the environment and spread like cancer to infest our everyday language. The philosopher Eric Hofer said, "Rudeness is the weak man's imitation of strength." Indeed, we must pity rude people: they try to hide weakness, sadness, and insecurity behind the masks of cruelty, lack of consideration, and rudeness. We cannot cure their sadness or anger but we have every right to require them to control their behavior and language at work.

We live in a rapidly changing world, but the old-fashioned values of politeness and kindness still offer the strongest armor for the warrior who seeks a true community. The great writer, Richard Wright, said, "I wish I had some way to make a bridge from man to man. . . ." Corporate policies matter, procedures matter, mentoring programs matter, but in the end it is language that makes the bridge from man to man . . . and people to people.

NONVERBAL ASPECTS OF A LANGUAGE OF COMMUNITY

Up until now we've mostly focused on verbal language, the words and sentences that link us together; but we also build or fail to build bridges nonverbally, with our eyes, our faces, our bodies, our silences, and our gestures.

First, I have to tell you about my grandson's ways of building community when he was eight months old. When he saw a new person, he didn't care about the person's color or nationality or size (although in all honesty he seemed to have a slight bias toward other babies and puppies), the price and style of clothing or job: all he cared about was genuine communication. If someone smiled at or talked to him, he smiled or, more accurately, gave a body smile and often reached out to touch the person's face. He understood the basic concept of seeking community in the midst of diversity.

And in the Geneva airport last year, in a place where varied cultures meet, we learned that all the other babies spoke the same language as our grandchild: human commonality, not diversity, links people to one another.

Endlessly fascinating, nonverbal communications pose singular problems for the diverse workforce. Nowhere does the secret code of nonverbal communications vex more than in the diverse workplace. Here are a few examples: the unwritten code for Mediterranean, Hispanic, and southern and eastern European cultures requires extensive touch and close proximity. When a French woman did her postdoctoral studies at IBM, she found that people constantly shied away from her: she followed the rules of a high-touch culture in the

United States, a low-touch, great-distance culture. In France and much of South America, you're expected to kiss business associates on both cheeks when you meet (some cultures require three kisses!); in the U.S., you might be accused of harassment. In the United States, it's considered a power gesture to put your feet up on the desk; showing the sole of the foot is a profound insult in parts of the Middle East. At a Hispanic professional meeting at which I spoke, a Puerto Rican man married to a WASP woman described the culture shock when they dined with each other's families at Christmas: his family all talked at once and gestured constantly; hers sat quietly and waited their turns to speak.

These nonverbal differences don't cause problems if we understand that what we're seeing is just a cultural difference. Our gestures don't reflect integrity, intelligence, or compassion—but some people think they do. In some situations, nonverbal attitudes learned at home fail to match the unspoken expectations at work and operate against employees' success or acceptance. Managers often tell me about these situations and indicate that they feel awkward mentioning them, so they remain silent, cheating the employee and possibly interfering with their career. We must speak the language that permits us to tell even painful truths, and to do so kindly.

What should our attitude be to differences in nonverbal behaviors at work? Embrace the differences and allow them to enrich our lives unless they cause problems or misunderstandings. If so, they're obstacles and must be dealt with. For example, some cultures teach youngsters to avert their eyes when speaking to authority figures, but at work, people are expected to make frequent eye contact: the employee who avoids eye contact may be seen as evasive or dishonest. Both the employee and the manager must explore and resolve the issue. People must learn to do what works and avoid what fails: such behavioral changes do not compromise one's integrity or cultural identity.

Do It Now!

If you have the sense that your diverse workplace isn't growing toward community, try videotaping a meeting and viewing the tapes to see whose nonverbal communications work and whose don't.

First Steps Toward a Global Language of Community

Feedback from students and colleagues as well as our own experiences abroad suggest that the ideas in this book lend themselves well to a worldwide language of community. Our global businesses pose many problems for us; language promises only small steps toward the dream of community. But they are steps in the right direction. Jennifer Hutchins, who brings the How to Say It ideas to consulting clients in Europe, Asia, and Latin America, reports that they travel well. Her comments follow, with a few words of mine added.

Business people I spoke to who work with diverse audiences agree that the most essential skill is adapting the message to the audience. In fact, people accustomed to multicultural settings might be more skilled at knowing their audiences than speakers who deal only with homogenous groups. The more often executives are forced to navigate cultural differences the more proficient they become at making their messages clear and concise to avoid misunderstandings.

In some cultures, such as in Japan or in the Middle East, the rules differ so much from ours that it's difficult to apply the communication tools we have learned. A woman living in Japan, for instance, told me that American businessmen often are taken advantage of there because they are too careful in following the mores. But some universal language principles elevate the success of an executive's speaking and writing.

Working as an international communications advisor during the past seven years, I have discovered that the effective communicator can apply the How to Say It principles almost anywhere. When in the global executive suite, business leaders understand their cultural bias without imposing it, feel proud of their nationality without flaunting it, and enthusiastic about their ethnicity without aggrandizing it. One vital principle is using precise and concise language. Statements that use too many "feel" words and "I" statements tend to evoke the stereotype of Americans as ethnocentric and egocentric. By sticking to the grammar principles, I have been able to gain the trust and support of audiences, whether they comprise Americans, Europeans, Asians, Latin Americans, or people from other backgrounds. I once held the position of project manager for a multicultural team based in Europe assigned to study the corporate culture of a global organization. At first my outsider status meant my leadership position met with resistance from the group members. But when I traded weak language for strong statements, my success increased. For example, I replaced statements such as "In the United States we think this method is effective" with "A proven method for researching company culture is xxx." Or "This type of message feels foreign to me" with "If we say it a different way, it should appeal to global audiences."

Keeping my messages clean of emotion and ethnocentric references has gone a long way in helping me to develop effective presentations and written messages. I often put together written material for international audiences and am always careful to use language free of jargon and insider cultural references.

In global settings, small turns of language can make enormous differences. Pay special attention to critical cases such as negotiating and decision-making. In these pressure situations people tend to fall back on the familiar. The key is to remember to use strong grammar, such as action verbs and parallelism and also to leverage silence. When people stumble over words they try to fill the pauses and this can distract from the message.

When I left Scandinavia, where I had lived and worked as an expatriate for two years, I presented a proposal to a high-level manager that would affect my professional and personal situation. The small group to which I presented were colleagues and also close friends and it was tempting to "get personal" and tell them why I wanted to work remotely as a consultant. Instead I set forth in PowerPoint the advantages of having an advisor abroad and conveyed my argument with powerful grammar. I countered objections with fact-backed sentences rather than emotional protests and made sure to exude confidence throughout the discussion, with strong posture and eye contact. At that point I also understood the language enough to throw in a few local phrases. Carefully chosen words and sentences enabled me to overcome cultural differences and turn the negotiation in my favor.[33]

DO NO HARM

Avoid putting your foot in your mouth in the first few minutes of your visit abroad. Read up on common mistakes people make and avoid them. Or simply ask one of your local associates to tell you what not to do and what is absolutely required (in France you kiss **both** cheeks).

AVOID MISUNDERSTANDING

In the global executive suite, the businessperson faces a high risk of being misinterpreted or misunderstood as a result of language and cultural differences. Focusing on the message rather than the messenger diminishes these hazards. Apparently innocent idioms and colloquialisms can cause fierce resistance to an executive's message. Sports and war metaphors such as "we'll run with the ball," "when we get to home base," and "bet the farm" can alienate multicultural audiences and add to the perception of Americans as coldly ambitious or closed minded.

TELL STORIES

The best stories are those to which all cultures can relate; for example, everyone appreciates stories about weddings and children. At a press conference with an audience of journalists from Denmark, the United Kingdom, Korea, China, and the United States, the story that struck a strong chord with all participants was not one of technology or manufacturing but of the entrepreneur who founded the company in the henhouse of a remote farm. It was a Cinderella story familiar to all.

---

[33]Hutchins, Jennifer, unpublished communication, October 14, 2003.

CLARIFY WITH VISUALS

Different pronunciations are overcome with clear visuals. Any word that could pose problems to the audiences will emerge if you write it on a handout, slide, or flip chart. Those chartjunk visuals we referred to earlier fail even more dismally with international audiences. Create clear visuals and handouts.

LEARN ABOUT THE CULTURE

Understanding something of the folklore, history, and sensitivities of your audience's culture is invaluable when preparing executive presentations. Referring to a popular local author or appropriate historical moments instantly endears people. It's not necessary to pretend you are an expert on Mexican history when you first present to an Hispanic culture. But it will mean a lot to your listeners if you show that you have bothered to research it. Also bother to learn the correct forms of address: Americans may prefer first names but many in the world prefer more formal modes of address. And be wary of insulting people: one executive visiting Ireland found himself in a pickle when he referred to John F. Kennedy's sexual adventures.

CHECK TRANSLATIONS

Run translated text by a native speaker. Don't accept the language-language dictionaries—they often don't cover idioms and yield bizarre "translations." In one example, the language-language dictionary translated "illusion" as "hallucination." The invitation read, "Come for the hallucinations," leading to the suspicion that drugs would be available. And a CEO employee newsletter on business innovation said, "All of us should be looking to try out new things in our lives; you should try this at home with your wife."

FIT THE GESTURES TO THE AUDIENCE

We all have heard tales of disastrous nonverbal language in international settings—the politician who offends an entire nation with a hand sign or a careless gesture that derails a negotiation. Sometimes, as in Asian cultures, protocol is so different from our own it's tempting to make a joke about being "an ugly American" and forget trying to follow the rules of bowing and gesturing. But with a little research and practice it's possible to keep gestures appropriate while maintaining powerful posture. When working in Japan, Jennifer made sure to maintain poise without opening her body too much or offending my listeners with extended eye contact, which is considered rude in that culture. On home territory, visitors and expatriates usually follow the host country's nonverbal protocol. Still, sometimes the host country's customs clash with home countries' standards. For example, many Asian and Middle Eastern cultures prohibit touch and eye contact between men and women, while some cultures expect bribes as standard business practice. As the one in the executive suite, you must negotiate which customs to bend while remaining true to your ethical principles.

MATCH CLOTHING STYLE

Dress and appearance can operate for or against the visiting executive. The first tapes of General Jay Garner in Iraq show him wearing a T-shirt as he addresses an audience of Iraqis wearing suits and ties. Despite American custom, most other countries have not adopted business casual. Show respect for the places you visit by adopting the preferred clothing style.

EXPLORE DIFFERING BUSINESS STYLES

Jen led a multicultural team in Denmark; it consisted of a Brit, two Danes, a Norwegian, and one American (Jen). The team was asked to study and define the culture of an international firm. Many possible research methodologies were on the table. After vigorous but meandering debate, Jen said, "Let's take a vote on the research method." A majority emerged during the vote but everyone returned to the debate anyway. Puzzled, Jen wondered why, after the vote had such a clear outcome, the debate continued. A colleague later explained that the team assumed that she'd called the vote for her own interest but the team still wouldn't take a decision till everyone agreed. This reflects a cultural difference in decision-making style that you must address if you're to function well.

Let's return to that baby. As you saw earlier, the only universal gesture, the one that's understood all over the world, is the smile: every baby knows it. We should know it too. This chapter showed how the principles of How to Say It *help* build bridges between people and cultures.

CONCLUSION

We've taken quite a trip together, from certainty to paradox, from the receptive skills of reading and listening to the expressive skills of speaking and writing, from self-absorbtion to engagement with others, from diversity to community, from the strictly local to the global. At each step you met ideas and practices to nurture success in the executive suite.

Finally, we end our story with Martin Luther King, Jr.'s words: "The end is reconciliation; the end is redemption; the end is the creation of the beloved community." Like King's dream, your communications seek the creation of the beloved community, at home, at work, and abroad. Language helps us transform the workplace from a diverse stew to a beloved community.

COMMUNICATION GUIDEPOSTS

You face the lifelong job of building the communication skills that bring success. Unlike other skill sets, language is never fully mastered. There's always room for growth. On the next pages, you'll find lists of the skills covered in each chapter of *How to Say It for Executives*. Use them as tools for self-evaluation, as sources of staff and peer evaluation, and as prods to future growth. Have a great trip!

	Novice	Apprentice	Master	Mentor
SEMINAL IDEAS				
See leadership as a developmental process				
Develop language skills to develop as a novice				
Language skills as an apprentice				
Language skills as a master				
Language skills as a mentor				
Embrace Janus paradoxes				
Ask crucial questions				

	Novice	Apprentice	Master	Mentor
Craft and use crib sheets				
Follow models				

LEADING YOUR SELF

	Novice	Apprentice	Master	Mentor
Recognize own moods and emotions				
Perceive effect of own moods and emotions on others				
Control and regulate verbal and body language to enhance leadership				
Express emotions and passions appropriately				
Tell the truth about self to self and others (when suitable)				
Keep diary of successful and unsuccessful encounters				
Learn and lead mindfully				
Welcome risk				
Learn from mistakes, gain self-confidence				
Evaluate own performance				
Observe how others respond to you				

	Novice	Apprentice	Master	Mentor
READING				
Apply the Power Reading system to clear your in-basket				
Scan and skim at 100,000 words a minute				
Seek structures				
Read efficiently on the screen				
Preread for speed, comprehension, retention				
Deep Read 10 percent of in-basket				
Synthesize				
Spar with writers				
Read what you abhor				
Build a reading community				
LISTENING				
Avoid inappropriate filters				
Overcome five barriers to effective listening				
Adjust frames to optimize listening				
"Listen" with the eyes				
Obey rules of the body language of listening				
Keep precise notes				
Apply other listening responses: repeat, empathize, clarify, probe				

	Novice	Apprentice	Master	Mentor
LEADING WITHOUT WORDS				
Dress appropriately for leadership role				
Avoid overdressing				
Avoid underdressing				
Touch with your eyes				
Sit like a leader				
Hold the head high				
Coordinate words and gestures				
Show sincerity				
Maintain control				
Touch others				
Select suitable trappings				
Model powerful body language				
Foster or discourage others' behavior through body language				
Value silence				
Acquire a repertoire of podium gestures				
Rest well				
Lay a strong foundation with the feet				

	Novice	Apprentice	Master	Mentor
Face the audience every time you speak				
Avoid damaging gestures				
Build silence into talks and speeches				
Correct vocal weaknesses				

TALKING LIKE A LEADER

	Novice	Apprentice	Master	Mentor
Analyze and avoid most "I" statements				
Ask three questions before speaking				
Avoid victimizing with "I" statements				
Check for positive and negative "you" statements				
Prefer "we" statements				
Shun intimacies				
Trim hedges				
Avoid self-demeaning hedges				
Prevent puny passives				
Control passive voice				
Prefer action verbs				
Use 6 persuasive techniques				
Add rhetorical tools to repertoire				

	Novice	Apprentice	Master	Mentor
Utter parallel and balanced sentences				
Enumerate for logic and clarity				
Group threes				
Clarify with similes and metaphors				
Alliterate when possible				
Shed puny, vague, long, and hackneyed words				
Use appropriate jargon				
Strip away from mumbo jumbo jargon				
BUILDING STURDY STRUCTURES				
Lead speeches and written pieces with 8 techniques				
Copy excellent leads				
Avoid self-destructive leads				
Vary forms of thesis statement				
Build internal logic with transitions, lookbacks, and topics				
End smartly: sum up, call to act, add unity				
ORGANIZING SPOKEN AND WRITTEN COMMUNICATIONS Plan quickly with The Organization System				

	Novice	Apprentice	Master	Mentor
ADDRESSING YOUR PUBLIC				
Speak effectively to large audiences				
Avoid common public speaking mistakes				
Shun dreary visuals				
DELIVERING SPEECHES THAT LEAD				
Learn varied approaches to scripts				
Prepare complete scripts, step by step				
Read scripts for power and persuasion				
Use techniques that foster strong endings				
Acquire the trappings of successful talks				
Nurture group presentations				
Case the room				
Arrive early				
Organize the podium				
Anticipate problems				
Stick to the schedule				
Handle time changes				
Adjust for audiences of thousands				

	Novice	Apprentice	Master	Mentor
COMMUNICATING WITH SMALL GROUPS AND INDIVIDUALS				
Craft meetings that work				
Foster participation from quiet members				
Discourage overbearing members				
Manage difficult people				
Lead positive, productive arguments				
Deliver humane, truthful, caring critiques				
Set educative experiences for future leaders				
Mentor with seven approaches				
Lead and inspire in times of crisis				
Avoid common examples of failed leadership				
WRITING LIKE A LEADER				
Acknowledge that e-mail lasts forever and reaches the world quickly				
Write the truth without "fighting words"				
Control the tone of all executive writing				
Deal with the seven "Cs" of executive writing: community, content, complexity, control, clarity, compression, and continuity				

	Novice	Apprentice	Master	Mentor
BRIDGING CULTURES: FIRST STEPS TOWARD A GLOBAL LANGUAGE OF COMMUNITY				
Use executive suite skills to nurture a community at work				
Prevent language that breeds animosity				
Build community through verbal and nonverbal language				
Discriminate between differences to celebrate and obstacles to alter				
Tailor the message to the audience				
Adapt behaviors to various cultures				
Apply the How to Say It executive principles in varied situations				
Respect the history and customs of others				
Show humility regarding your way versus their way				
Avoid misunderstanding and poor impressions				
Tell stories				
Clarify with visuals				
Check for translation bloopers				
Fit the gestures to the audience				

	Novice	Apprentice	Master	Mentor
Match style to cultural norms				
Seek "reconciliation, redemption," and "creation of the beloved community"				
Grow from novice to mentor in all aspects of communications				

INDEX

Abrams, Evelyn, 15
Action verb, 134, 151
  grammatical use of, 66–67, 69, 79
  purpose of, 102–103
Active voice
  grammatical use of, 66
  transforming to, 67
Aggressive reading, 28
Albertini, Kathleen Barry, 22
Ali, Muhammad, 53
Aliterates, 19
Allen, Woody, 22
Alliteration, rhetorical use of, 77
American culture, 36
Anderson, Hans Christian, 129
Anger, sentences that show, 79
Animosity, language creating, 158
Apprentice, 138
  characteristics of, 3
  communication skills of, 4
  definition of, 3
  development of, 4
Arizona State University, 70
Ash, Mary Kay, 1
Assessment
  benefits of self, 13
  from outside sources, 13
Audience, 94

considerations for, 102, 108
diversity in, 163
relaxing of, 112
written communications for, 146
Audiovisual, 121
Authority, 72
Automaton, 15
Axtell, Roger, 52

Baker, Sheridan, 74
Balance, rhetorical use of, 75
Barriers, to listening, 31, 33–35
  experiments in, 43
  filters as, 33
  inaccuracy as, 34
  inattention as, 34
  mismatches as, 34
  one listening style as, 35
Barzun, Jacques, 142
Bennis, Warren, vii, 5, 12
Berlin, Isiah, 31
The Bible, 89
Billings, Josh, 89
Blair, Tony, 61, 63, 74, 75, 77, 141
Body language, 31, 46, 120, 134
  of leader, 51
  leadership presence in, 46
  listening and attending to, 36

Body Politics (Henley), 55
Bohr, Niels, 6
Bottom-up method, 103
Braille, 20
Brooks, Renana, 61
Burns, James MacGregor, 125
Bush, George W., 14, 35, 140

Call to action, presentation for, 98
Capital letters, inappropriate use of, 144
Carter, Stephen, 31, 32, 41
Casarett, Vicki, 55, 57
Challenges, of leadership, 2
Chamberlain, Neville, 88
Charisma, 49, 50, 126
Chartjunk, 166
Chase, Stuart, 160
Checklist, communications guidepost with, 171–180
Churchill, Winston, 63, 69, 89, 101
Cialdini, Robert, 70, 72, 135
Civil argument, 130
Civil language, 134
Civil listening, 32
Civil war, 68
Clarity, 155
    written communications for, 147, 150–152
Cleanliness, 48
Clinton, William Jefferson, 13–14, 87, 98
Code of reciprocity, 71
Commitment, 71
Communication
    of apprentice, 4
    email, 143
    improving, 145
    leadership with, 1
    of master, 4–5
    of mentor, 5–6
    mistakes of, 143
    of novice, 3
    organized, 101–102
    tone altering, 145
Communication Frames, 31, 35–36
Communications, 94
Community, 154, 157
    written communications for, 146
Complexity, 154
    written communications for, 147
Compression, 155
    written communications for, 151–152
Confrontational listening, 41
Content, 154
    written communications for, 147

Continuity, written communications for, 152–153
Control, 154
    written communications for, 149–150
Conventions, 21, 22, 23
Cook, Jeff Scott, 116
Creative reasoning, 104
Crib sheets, *how to say it,* 10
Criticize, sentences that, 79
Critiques
    action verbs in, 134
    body language of, 134
    delivering, 133–135
    precise language of, 134
    proper words for, 134
    recipient addressed by, 134
    strengths addressed in, 135
Crusade, 35, 140
Cultural differences
    language with, 157–158, 165
    nonverbal communications for, 161–163
Curie, Marie, 19

Declaration of Independence, 76, 77
Decorative structures, 85
Deep reading
    considerations of, 24
    example of notes for, 26
    exercises in, 30
    instrument of leadership, 25
    techniques of, 24
    technologies influence on, 24
Demeanor, effects of, 16
Depression, 15–16
Dewey, John, 137
Diary, 17
Difficult people, approaches for, 128
Diversity, audience of, 163
Donnellon, Ann, 6

Effective listening, 35
Einstein, Albert, 148
Eisenhower, Dwight D., 99
Ellis, Havelock, 90
Email, appropriate use of, 143
Emerson, Ralph Waldo, 4, 90
Emotional intelligence, 14
Empathetic listening, 35, 41
Empathy, 41
End structures, isolating of, 117
Endings, presentation for, 98–99
Enumeration, 96
    rhetorical use of, 75

Expression, in listening, 31
Extended metaphors, 76
Eye contact, 46, 162, 167
   defined, 51
   leadership presence using, 46
   listening behaviors using, 39

Failure, 12–13
Fear, 12–13, 15
Filters
   as barriers to listening, 33–34
   checklist of, 34
   prejudice as, 33–34
Flagging pages, 25
Flanders and Swann, 53

Gardner, Howard, 1, 2, 5, 12, 25, 137
Garner, Jay, 167
Geneen, Harold, 89
Gerstner, Louis V., Jr., 90
Gestures, 46, 50, 55, 114, 161–162
Gestures: The do's and taboos of body language around the world (Axtell), 52
The Gettysburg Address, 61
Giuliani, Rudolph, 140
Goals, 111
Goldilocks, 146
Goleman, Daniel, 14
Goodman, Ellen, 70
Gorbachev, Mikhail, 13
Grammar
   action verb used in, 66–67, 69, 79
   active voice in, 66
   authority influenced by, 58–61
   "I" statements in, 58–61
   object in, 66
   parallelism in, 74
   passive voice in, 66
   state-of-being verb in, 69
   subject in, 66
   transitive verbs in, 66
Grammar checker, 150
Grant, Ulysses S., 68
Guideposts, 3, 4, 11, 155
   communications checklist, 171–180

Handouts, 114
Hannon, Kathryn, 7
Hedging
   defined, 64
   examples of, 64–65
   questions in, 65

Henley, Nancy, 55
Hills, Carla, 88
Hofer, Eric, 160
Horace, 160
"How Management teams Can Have a Good Fight" (Eisenhardt, Kahwajy, Bouregeois), 129
How to Say It, 31, 40, 126, 163
   crib sheets, 10
How To Say It For Women (Mindell), 2
Human expressiveness, 49
Hussein, Saddam, 75
Hutchins, Jennifer, 163

"I" statements, 164
   gaining control of, 62, 127, 129, 140
   leadership statements transformed from, 58–61
IBM, 161
Ideas, development of, 1
Illiteracy, 19
Image consultant, 48
Inaccuracy, as barriers to listening, 34
Inattention, as barriers to listening, 34
Inspire, sentences that, 78
Instructions
   absolute, 16
   conditional, 16
Internal structures
   topic sentences for, 96–97
   transitions in, 96–97
Interruptions, 122

Janus paradoxes, 6–7, 35, 50, 53, 61, 67
Jargon, 80, 102
Johnson, Lyndon, 95
Jokes, 160
Judgment, scarcity influencing, 73

Kennedy, Florynce, 116
Kennedy, John F., 31, 75, 78, 99, 116
Keynote speaker, 120
Keystone structure, 93–94
King, Martin Luther, Jr., 19, 61, 74, 75, 76, 77, 90, 100, 168

Lacy, Dan, 18
Langer, Ellen, 16
Language
   animosity created from, 158
   appropriateness in, 160
   cultural differences in, 157–158
   effective grammatical structure in, 9–10
   leadership with, 95, 129

Language (*cont.*)
　leadership's influence from, 4, 69
　negative, 59
　positive responses through, 71
　principles of, 9–11
　rhetoric in, 73–74
　self shaping, 12
　studies of, 34–35
　successful use of, 140–141
　transitional phrases used in, 10
　weak use of, 140
Language of community, 157
Larsen, Doug, 34
Lead
　presentation opening, 86
　sentences that, 77
Leadership. *See also* Nonverbal leadership
　adjusting to circumstances of, 8
　challenges of, 2
　communication in, 1, 3–6
　crisis overcome by, 139
　deep readings influence on, 25
　ethics of, 8
　growth in, 17
　language of, 95, 129
　models use in, 10
　nurturing skills of, 138
　paradoxes of, 6–7
　persuasiveness in, 101
　presence, 46
　readings role in, 18–29
　requirements of style for, 46
　statement, 60
　styles of, 8, 27
　synthesis's role in, 26
　workday in, xvii
Leadership (Burns), 125
Leadership ability, writing's challenges of,
　　153–154
Leadership communications, universal approach to,
　156
Leadership development
　of apprentice, 3–4
　of master, 4–5
　of mentor, 5–6
　of novice, 2–3
　stages of, 2–6
Leading Minds (Gardner), 1, 25
Learning, mindful, 16
Lebowitz, Fran, 89
Leder, Phil, 138
Leno, Jay, 153

Lieberman, Joseph, 156
Lightening bugs, 79–80, 84
Lightening words, 79–80, 84
Lincoln, Abraham, 19, 74, 89, 90, 139, 141
Listening
　barriers to, 31, 33–35
　body language in, 36
　defined, 31
　expressions in, 31
　how not to, 32
　importance of, 31
　reception in, 31
　value of, 32
Listening behaviors
　checklist of, 38
　eye contact in, 39
　gestures in, 39
　note taking for, 39
　open body in, 37
　showing, 37
　visibility for, 37
Listening experiments, 40–42
Listening situations, experiments in, 43–45
Listening stance, 43–45
Listening technique, 43–45
Little, Royal, 89

Mahaffy, John, 89
Malcolm X, 19, 99
Manguel, Alberto, 18
Marginalia, 28
　defined, 27
Margins, 155
Marked text
　purpose of, 25
　techniques, 25
Mason, Jackie, 90
Master, 137
　traits of, 5
McPherson, James, 68
Meeting environment, checklist for, 126
Mentor, 4, 30, 137
　origins of, 5
　traits of, 5
Metaphor, 35, 165
　rhetorical use of, 76
"Microbe Hunters," 19
Miller, Laura, 24
Mindell, Phyllis, 106
Mindlessness, 16
Mismatches, as barriers to listening, 34
Mistakes, 13–14

Mitchell, Richard, 58
Mix, Ron, 55
Model sentences, 77
Models, leaderships use of, 10
Moderator, 122
Moral courage, 68, 69

Nader, Ralph, 89
Naisbitt, John, 89
Negative language, 59
Negotiating
    admired for, 135–136
    authorities influence in, 136
    behaviors for successful, 136–137
    consistency in, 136
    reciprocity in, 136
    scarcity in, 136
    situations comparable in, 136
Negotiation, 71
The New York Times, 21, 45, 140
No, sentence saying, 78
Nonverbal communications, 36, 46, 123
    cultural differences in, 161–163
Nonverbal leadership
    behavior influenced by, 54
    body opened in, 50
    control maintained by, 53
    dress appropriately for, 54
    eyes touching with, 51
    fifteen principles of, 50–54
    gestures in, 52
    head held high for, 52
    it's not about you, 50
    as model for behavior, 54
    reaching out with, 53
    silence with, 54
    sincerity with, 53
    sitting as, 51
    smiling as, 52
Novice, 137, 138
    communication skills of, 3
    perspectives of, 2–3
    traits of, 2
Numerical relationships, 114
Nurture
    leadership skills that, 138
    sentences that, 78

Object, grammatical use of, 66
Odyssey, 5
One listening style, as barriers to listening, 35
Organization system, 102–105, 107, 115, 146, 155

Palm Pilot, 32
Paradoxes
    of leadership, 6–7
    list of, 7–8
Parallelism, 152
    improving writing with, 152
    rhetorical use of, 74
Paraphrasing, 21, 40–41
Passive reading, 28
Passive voice, 143
    examples of, 68
    grammatical use of, 66
    transforming from, 67
Personalization, 61
Persuasion, 72, 86, 91, 144
    leadership with, 101
    techniques for, 4, 10, 70
Persuasive process, titles in, 153–154
Podium, organizing, 121
Podium gestures
    animation with, 56
    arms opening in, 56
    audience facing towards, 56
    palm pointing with, 56
    resting position in, 55
    silence in, 56
    worst gestures avoided in, 56
Pope Paul VI, 87
Positive listening, 37
Positive responses, creating, through language,
    71–73
Posture, 46, 51
Power reading, 21, 22
Precise listening, 39
Precise reading, 39
Precise words, 160, 164
Precision listening, 35
Precision reading, 21
Prereading, 22–24
    deep reading in, 24
    defined, 23
    exercises in, 30
    four steps of, 23–24
    structure for, 23
    thesis statement in, 23
    topics in, 23–24
Presentation
    anecdote for, 88
    avoidance in, 93
    call to action in, 98
    common experience for, 90
    conclusion of, 97–100

Presentation (*cont.*)
  dressing for, 119
  evaluation of, 123–124
  host gratitude for, 87
  host references for, 87
  introduction of, 86–93
  leading, 86–89
  summing up of, 98
Presentation planning
  audience considered in, 108
  details grouped for, 109–110
  details listed for, 108–109
  details sequenced for, 110
  planned and completed for, 112–113
  problem anticipation for, 121–122
  purpose of, 108
  quotation for, 88–90
  rehearsing for, 114
  speaking rate of, 113, 117
  speech overview for, 87
  strong endings in, 98–99
  summing up, 98
  topics named for, 110–111
  topics sequenced for, 111
  verb uses in, 108
  visual aids for, 114
  word relevant for, 90–91
Probe, 42
Pronouns, 62
Psychological barriers, 86
Public speaking, 106, 120
  creativity in, 57
  examples of, 106
  gestures for, 55
  improving, 13–14
  resting position for, 55
Punctuation, meaning changed by, 149

Queen of England, 140
Quotation marks, 149

Ravitch, Diane, 89
Read aloud, 118
Reading, 21, 22. *See also* Deep reading
  availability of materials for, 19
  developing relationships in, 26–27
  exercises in, 28, 30
  improving, 20, 29
  leadership and role of, 18–29
  playing devil's advocate in, 28
  problems with, 19–20
  scanning in, 21– 23

  skimming in, 21–23
  techniques from childhood in, 20
Reagan, Ronald, 13, 71, 77
Reception, in listening, 31
References, 150
Repetition, 40–41
Required structures, 85
Resting position, in public speaking, 55
Retention, 111
Rhetoric, 91, 104
  alliteration in, 77
  balance in, 75
  enumeration in, 75
  languages use of, 73–77
  metaphor in, 76
  parallelism in, 74
  rhetorical question in, 75–76
  simile in, 76
  tricolon in, 76
Rhetorical question, rhetorical use of, 75–76
Ridge, Tom, 153
Rifkin, Glenn, 45
Risk, 4, 12
Roosevelt, Eleanor, 12
Roosevelt, Franklin D., 87
Rudeness, 161

Safir, William, 77
Salon.com, 24
Sapir, Edward, 46, 49
Sartre, Jean-Paul, 18
Scanning, reading with, 21–23
Scarcity, judgment influenced by, 73
Schulman, Paul, 7
Scientists, nobel laureate, 18–19
Screening groups, 29
Script, preparation of, 116–118
Search engines, 21
Self awareness
  attaining, 14–15
  characteristics of, 14–15
  inadequate, 15
Self confidence, 13–14
Self regulation, 14–16
  mindful learning, 16
Self understanding, 15
Self-awareness, 27
Self-introductions, 40
Self-regulation, 27
Sentence forms, 91, 96
  weak use of, 63
Sentence starters, 40–41, 118

Sentence structure
   improved clarity in, 148
   improving, 81–84
Sentences
   anger in, 79
   credit given by, 127
   criticizing, 79
   inspiring, 78
   leading, 77
   nurturing, 78
   participation discouraged by, 127
   participation encouraged by, 127
   say no, 78
   topic sentences for, 23, 96–97, 113
Sequence, 110–111
Seven c's of writing, written communications with,
   145–154
Shakespeare, William, 12
Silence, 46
Simile, rhetorical use of, 76
Skimming
   reading with, 21–23
   techniques of, 22
Slides, 114
Social psychologists, 70
Social validation, 72
Speaking. See Public speaking
Speed reading, 20
The Speed and power reading system, 20
State-of-being verb, grammatical use, 69
Stevenson, Robert Louis, 104
Structures, 97
   benefits of, 100
   internal, 96–97
   presentation conclusion in, 97–100, 112–113
   presentation introduction in, 86–93, 112–113
   reading, 30
   thesis statement, 93–96, 112
Style, 46
   appropriate, 47
   essentials of, 48
   inappropriate, 47–48
   leaderships requirements of, 46
Subject, grammatical use of, 66
Success, 12
Summarize, 153
Summing up, presentation, 98
Sycophants, 137
Synthesis, 25–26, 104
   defined, 26
   importance of, 27
   in leadership strategy, 26

the Taliban, 75
Team performance, 120
Team Talk (Donnellon), 6
Technology, influence on deep reading, 24
Text-marking, 24, 117
The Emperor's New Clothes (Anderson),
   129
Thesis, 27
Thesis statement, 23, 93, 96, 112, 123
   practicing, 94
Tilghman, Shirley, 138
Titanic, 146
Tithenai, defined, 26
Titles, persuasive process with, 153–154
Tone, communication altered by, 145
Top-down method, 103
Topic sentences, 23, 96–97, 113
   internal structures for, 96–97
Topics, 27
Touch, 46
Transcript analysis, 130
Transitional phrases, 96–97
Transitional words, 96–97
Transitions, internal structures for, 96–97, 113
Transitive verbs, 66
Tricolon, 105
   rhetorical use of, 76
Truman, Harry, 12
Tufte, Edward, 150
Tufte's, Edward, 114
Twain, Mark, 79
Tzu, Lao, 90

Universal approach, leadership communications
   with, 156

Vendler, Helen, 27, 148
Verb
   action, 66
   passive to active, 67
   presentation use of, 108
   state of being, 69
   transitive, 66
Verbal response, 43–45
Video camera, 121
Videotape, 17, 19, 49, 57, 118, 119, 130, 133
Vietnam war, 95
Vigor, writing with, 152
Visual aids, 96, 105, 114
Visual and Statistical Thinking (Tuft), 150
Vocabulary, 34
Volunteering, 4

The Wall Street Journal, 21
War and Peace, 22
"We" statements, 62–63
Well-Read's leadership seminars, 14, 159
White, E.B., 85
Will to act, 69
World Wide Web, 19, 21–22, 24
    research of, 91
Wright, Richard, 161
Writing
    leadership's challenges of, 153–154
    vigor in, 152

Written communications
    appropriate language in, 145
    audience in, 146
    clarity in, 147, 150–152
    community in, 146
    complexity in, 147
    content in, 147
    continuity in, 152–153
    control in, 149–150
    seven c's of, 145–154

Yalow, Rosalind, 19
"You" statements, 62

ABOUT THE AUTHOR

The dean of a medical school called her "the world's expert on professional communications." Dr. Phyllis Mindell founded and leads Well-Read (wel'-red'), international communications consultants, and serves as adjunct professor at Georgetown University Medical School. Her books, *Power Reading* (selected as one of the thirty best business books of the year); *A Woman's Guide to the Language of Success;* and *How to Say It for Women,* have been translated into German, Chinese, and Arabic. She and her work have been featured in *The New York Times*, Gannett Newspapers, *Bloomberg Business*, and dozens of newspapers, magazines, and television programs in the United States and abroad.

A popular speaker, she keynotes and addresses national and international conferences, including Department of Agriculture; Simmons; State of Texas, State of Pennsylvania, University of Rochester, Bryant College Leadership Summits; Association of American Medical Colleges; University of Michigan Medical School; and Chautauqua Institution.

She holds a doctorate from the University of Rochester, a Master's degree from City University of New York, and a Bachelor's degree from Brooklyn College. Her postdoctoral studies include neurolinguistics, writing, and literature.

She and Marvin, her husband of forty-six years, live and work in Rochester, N.Y., and Washington, D.C. Their children, Ossie Borosh, Joe, and David, and their grandchildren, Arye and Samuel, light up their lives.

About Well-Read (Wel'-Red')

With the help of its Family of Experts, Well-Read designs and presents professional and executive seminars on how to lead, read, write, speak, listen, and cross cultural boundaries. Clients come from nearly every country and many large and small companies, universities, and professional groups. Well-Read's client list includes General Mills; Solvay Minerals; Xerox; Corning; McKinsey; the medical schools of Harvard, University of California, and Michigan; PriceWaterhouseCoopers; UBS; Motorola; Xerox European Research Centre (France) as well as other large and small companies and nonprofit institutions worldwide.

Well-Read's Web site offers detailed program information as well as educational articles and book reviews.

You can reach Well-Read and Dr. Phyllis Mindell at:

Phone: 800 245 0806

E-mail: pmindell@well-read.com

Web site: www.well-read.com